How to Become

a Good Dancer

by ARTHUR MURRAY

with Dance Secrets by KATHRYN MURRAY

illustrated by LEALAND GUSTAVSON

SIMON AND SCHUSTER, NEW YORK · 1954

LIBRARY OF CONGRESS CATALOG CARD NUMBER: 54-5895
DEWEY DECIMAL CLASSIFICATION NUMBER: 793.3
MANUFACTURED IN THE UNITED STATES OF AMERICA
PRINTED BY KONECKY ASSOCIATES
BOUND BY H. WOLFF BOOK MFG. CO., INC.

Table of Contents

PART THREE *The Waltz and Its Variations*

PART FOUR *The Latin American Dances*

PART FIVE *Swing*

PART SIX *Dance Secrets,*
by KATHRYN MURRAY

PART SEVEN *Dancing for Children*

The Art of Dancing

THE FIRST THING I would like to give you is a clear, definite answer to the question: "Just what *is* Dancing?"

Some beginners seem to feel that Dancing is entirely a series of exercises or a footwork routine. Others at first think of Dancing as either an exhibition or a self-betrayal—that a Man and Girl step on the dance floor, and either win glory for themselves as a skilled team, or reveal themselves as a fumbling, unhappy couple.

But neither of these conceptions gives a true picture of Dancing. Actually (and I want you always to keep this in mind)— *Dancing is "conversation" to music!*

When you dance, you express yourself. You hold your partner's interest through the correct use of musical rhythm, just as in good conversation you hold another's interest through use of the spoken word.

As you dance, each correctly timed step is like a well-chosen remark. It shows your partner that you "know what it's all about." And just as a speaking knowledge of many things makes you a more interesting talker, *a dancing knowledge* of a variety of steps makes you a more attractive dancer. The more skill you acquire, the more "words" you will have with which to converse.

You know that the foreigner who has not learned the English

language has difficulty in making himself understood. He is so busy trying to *think* of the right words that he stammers and hesitates.

And so it is with dancing. If you are too busy *thinking* about each step—if you are uncertain and timid—you certainly can't express yourself freely. There will be too many things on your mind for you to be yourself. And being yourself—gracefully, rhythmically—is the whole secret of good dancing.

To be a good dancer, you must be able to dance without having to concentrate on the steps. Your feet must have learned to respond easily and smoothly to the music. You must be able to lead or follow without apparent effort. And this final stage of perfection is reached in only one way: Practice—practice—and *more practice!*

I have arranged the instructions in this book so you will have no difficulty in progressing from one easy step to another to become a good dancer in a very short time.

But before we begin, I want to add a very important warning: Do not skip any of the material in the early lessons just because it looks easy, or boring. You will need the groundwork in order to carry on; without the basic instructions, you will have trouble learning the more advanced steps. Even if you have danced before, review the preliminary steps—don't start in the middle.

You are now ready to take your first step!

ARTHUR MURRAY

How to Become a Good Dancer

PART ONE

THE FIRST STEP

The Walking Step or One Step

> Read this whole chapter through first, before you try any practicing at all. Then go back to the beginning and practice the step as instructed.

THE WALKING STEP is the easiest of all steps so we will start with it. Known as the One Step, it was the first of the modern dances to become popular. The One Step came into vogue in this country back in 1912 and is still in use.

It has undergone no essential change since then. Here is what Vernon Castle had to say about it:

> Bear in mind this one important point—when I say *walk,* that is all it is. Simply walk as softly and as smoothly as possible, taking a step to every count of the music.
>
> This is the One Step, and this is all there is to it. There are many different figures [after you have mastered the step], but they are all in the same strict tempo. It is simply *one* step taken to each beat of the music—hence its name.

The One Step today remains a simple, brisk walk, taken very much in the same way that soldiers march. Regardless of other factors, the whole trick is simply *to take one walking step to each count,* just as if you were marching along in a parade.

We now go on to consider this walking step in detail.

Here is exactly how the step is danced:

REMEMBER THESE {

1. The walking step is brisk.
2. Rise on your toes before you start.
3. Don't slide, scrape, shuffle, or hug the floor with your feet.
4. Walk noiselessly. When in motion, lift your feet about a quarter of an inch.
5. The length of your step should be about twelve to fifteen inches.

Now I am going to ask you to practice this step on the floor. At this preliminary stage of the game, both Men and Girls are to try the step walking *forward,* although, as you will very soon see, Girls have to learn to walk backward since that is their normal step in dancing. (Men will have to walk backward sometimes, but Girls will nearly always do so.)

Practicing the Walking Step Forward

Remember the characteristics of the step in the five points just given above. Now try this:

PRACTICE

1. Reach far forward with the toes of your *left* foot—but reach naturally. Don't try to take an enormous stride. Reach from the hip, keeping your left knee straight, but not exaggeratedly stiff. Step out just as if you were marching.
2. The toes of your left foot should touch the floor first. This is a dance—not a goose step.
3. Then swing your right foot forward, knee straight, toes touching the floor first.
4. Keep on walking ahead, repeating the step.

15

ALL RIGHT NOW, LET'S GO!

But first go back to the beginning of this chapter and read it over again, practicing the actual step this time at the places marked PRACTICE. And practice doesn't mean doing it just once or twice.

Practice the step over and over again until your feet remember it.

Then when you come to this part of the chapter on your second way through, you will be ready to do some real practicing, for you are now going to—

PRACTICE

Practice the One Step while you sing aloud the first two lines of "Yankee Doodle."

Start off, walking forward with your left foot first (Men and Girls both), and take one step on each of the first *capitalized* words or syllables. Like this:

> YANK-ee DOOD-le CAME to TOWN
> a-RID-ing ON his PO-NY
> STUCK a FEATH-er IN his HAT
> and CALLED it MAC-a-RO-NI

Step out briskly and you'll find that it's fun!

And Girls—don't forget to practice walking backward, starting off with the right foot.

Why I Teach You the One Step First

You may wonder why I am first teaching you the One Step since it is a dance step that is now seldom used by itself. You are not likely to have much opportunity to go out on the dance floor and actually make use of this simple step as such. But it is an important basic step—from it the Fox Trot is evolved, and it is in itself necessary as one of the combinations from which many other steps can be made up.

As a matter of fact, the actual term "One Step" has fallen into disuse, because the Fox Trot played twice as fast is the same as the One Step. Consequently most phonograph records are not stamped with the label "One Step."

But the One Step (quick walking step) may be danced to any fast Fox Trot music.

This is just for your information. Don't worry about music at this point.

How to Develop
Your Dancing Form

NOW THAT we have covered the One Step in detail, I have a few general topics of importance that I want to take up with you before going on to the Fox Trot.

By now you will see the general organizational plan of these instructions. I give you general information in order to build up your knowledge of the art of dancing. And then I give you specific instructions so that you will be able to learn the actual steps.

This general information is important. There is more to the art of dancing than just being able to move your feet properly.

THE LINE OF DIRECTION

Obviously every dance floor, no matter how big, must have its limits. You can't go on walking in a straight line forever, and there has to be some generally accepted convention or there would be confusion with everyone dancing every which way, bumping into one another.

In street traffic motorists have to keep to the right. So in dancing there is a regular rule for direction.

The Line of Direction is the direction dancers should follow in their progress around the room. Even while you are learning you might just as well acquire the right habit now—the habit you will need when you first step out in a ballroom.

The Line of Direction Is Always Counter-clockwise.

This simply means that you go around the room in the direction *opposite* to that which the hands of a clock take in traveling around the face.

You can always remember this by simply imagining that there is a clock in the middle of the room, lying face up on the floor. Go forward in the direction *opposite* to the way the hands move.

START

PRACTICE

Now try practicing the One Step around the room, *always going in the Line of Direction.*

Learn this habit now, for you will always need it. Not following the Line of Direction is like "going against the grain"—you are bound to run into other couples on the floor unless you go in the Line of Direction.

The Secret of Walking Correctly

MEN AND GIRLS face different ways on the actual dance floor. They must both learn how to walk correctly.

I start off with the Man's instructions since they are simpler.

MAN'S INSTRUCTIONS:

Remember that the Man normally walks *forward* most of the time in dancing—the Girl steps backward.

Consequently the Man always starts off with his *left* foot first (and the Girl with her right foot, so the two partners are always in step together).

When you dance:

Lift your feet slightly off the floor when walking, do not let them drag or scrape on the floor.

Do not let your heels touch the floor *at all* when you are dancing backward. When you are walking forward, you may let your heels touch the floor.

Always move naturally, easily, comfortably. Don't strain, don't exaggerate the steps, and don't be self-conscious.

To give spring to your steps, practice rising up and down on your toes, taking long slow walking steps around the room in the Line of Direction.

GIRL'S INSTRUCTIONS:

Remember that the Girl normally walks backward most of the time—the Man steps forward.

Consequently the Girl will always start backward with her

right foot (and the Man forward with his left, so the two partners are always in step together).

If you want to dance well, you first have to learn to step well. When you dance:

Learning to step backward properly not only teaches the Girl how to keep her feet out of her partner's way—but it will also improve her appearance on the dance floor.

You always begin with your right foot and take long steps backward. The toe of your backward-moving foot should go back as far as possible. Practice an extremely long step.

The Girl whose long steps have become second nature can follow any lead twice as easily as the Girl who takes short steps. And—by taking long steps you will protect your feet from being stepped on.

After taking a long step backward you will always be ready for the next step.

THIS POSITION IS WRONG

It is absolutely impossible for a girl to dance well when her feet are placed flat on the floor. In this position her steps will be short and her partner will be unable to strike out with a long, free, easy dancing stride.

Not only will she be a heavy handicap to her partner, but her feet will appear large and clumsy on the floor.

22

THIS POSITION IS RIGHT

Note that when the toes lead, a girl's step becomes long and free moving and that her foot looks graceful.

Here is an easy trick: imagine that you want to point the way in every step with your one big toe. Let it lead whichever way you move. REACH WITH YOUR TOE, stretching from the ankle—not from the hip.

REVIEW

Now FOR a brief review and you'll be ready to practice the One Step by yourself. Remember that:

The Line of Direction is always *counter-clockwise*.

The Man's *right* hand and the Girl's *left* will be near the wall when walking in their normal steps in the Line of Direction.

Both Man and Girl should practice the One Step forward at first, just because that is the simplest way.

The Man should keep in mind that he will normally be walking forward.

The Girl should remember that she will be walking backward most of the time—and she should start to practice that way as soon as she has grasped the elements of the step.

The Man always starts off with the *left* foot.

The Girl always starts off with the *right* foot (when going backward).

IMPORTANT

No man should ever make the mistake of thinking that if the *girl* knows the steps, she can help guide him around the floor. *The man should always lead,* and lead correctly.

No girl should ever make the mistake of thinking that if the *man* knows the steps, she can "get by" through simply following what he does. This attitude has made poor dancers out of thousands of girls who could just as easily, and far more enjoyably, be good dancers.

Always remember: If you can dance well alone, you can then dance more easily and successfully with a partner. Practice in private—to be popular in public!

Why Girls Must Also Know the Steps

Whenever I hear a woman say, "All I need is a good leader," I know that she is probably a poor dancer and that partners steer clear of her.

"Leading" must be a misleading word—so many girls confuse it with "dragging"! The leader is merely the one who chooses the steps and guides his partner into them. But, unless his partner is *alert* and ready to dance with him, she merely becomes an extra weight to be carried around.

A girl cannot dance *with* her partner until she knows what she is doing. She can test her own knowledge by trying to dance alone to music or by leading a girl partner. If she feels helpless by herself, she can tell immediately that she does not know her own part. It will be safer for her to refuse invitations until she has learned what she needs to make her popular and fun to have as a partner.

Once a girl becomes interested in the steps themselves, she will enjoy learning. She will begin to notice dancing technique on the stage, the screen and among her friends. The more steps a girl knows, the more spontaneity she will show in her dancing.

Three Secrets That Will Help a Girl to Become a Good Dancer

1. Learn lightness—it is vital—and to do this you must practice in order to strengthen the muscles used in dancing.

2. Learn to do the basic steps alone. Then when you are on the actual dance floor you will know what your partner is doing, and you will not discourage him by depending on him for support.

3. Learn a variety of steps. You can follow properly only as many steps as you *know*, and the strongest leader can't make you follow steps that are unfamiliar to you.

I can't stress too often or too emphatically the importance of learning to dance independently of your partner.

How to Keep Time to Music
and Develop Your Sense of Rhythm

There is a mistaken impression that it is necessary to be able to "carry a tune" in order to learn how to keep time to music. This unfortunate belief keeps many people from learning to dance.

The ability to carry a tune is not a necessary factor in learning to dance. To dance, you must simply be able *to keep time to music*. And if you can march to band music, or if your foot can beat time to ordinary dance music, you have a good enough sense of rhythm to enjoy dancing.

Everyone was born with a sense of rhythm. Forget that you must know music—nine out of ten dancers don't know one note from another, yet they can keep time.

IF YOU CAN CARRY A TUNE:

If you can sing, hum, or whistle a tune—*any* tune, whether it is a popular dance number, a nursery lullaby or "Yankee Doodle" —then you have already proved that you have sufficient rhythm to become a good dancer.

IF YOU CAN'T CARRY A TUNE:

Remember this: dancers do not keep time to the melody or the tune of a song. The high and low notes have nothing to do with it. The count in dancing is determined by the *beat* or tempo of the music.

If you are standing at the curb when a parade band passes by, you automatically *feel* the beat and tempo of the march being played. The "oompah-oompah" of the big brass horns and the "boom, boom, boom-boom-boom" of the big bass drum arouse in you a regular, rhythmic *pulse*. Your muscles automatically get ready to swing you off in perfect step with the rest of the parade!

The same principle is true of dance music. When you hear a popular song played on the radio or phonograph, you cannot help feeling the underlying tempo, or beat, or pulse, of the music. If an orchestra is playing, this beat is usually carried by the bass drum. As you listen, shut your eyes and visualize the drummer's foot working the pedal of that drum. At each beat his foot goes down, and a soft "boom" accents the tempo.

These accented or "boom" beats are all you need for dancing. To make sure that you recognize them (if there still is any question in your mind), do these two things:

1. Beat Time With Your Foot.

Sit next to your radio or phonograph and listen to any dance music. Imagine that you are the drummer and simply beat time with your foot on the floor as though you were hitting the pedal of the bass drum. Tap your hand on the chair arm at the same time. Keep tapping to different types of music until it becomes automatic to follow the drum beat.

2. Walk in Time to Music.

After you have learned to beat time, walk around the room, taking one step to each beat. Do this in private, so that you will not feel self-conscious. Try walking to several different songs. In a surprisingly short while, your feet will "carry the tune" easily.

And that's all there is to keeping time with the music!

In following chapters I will tell you how this applies to each dance; but the same simple principle applies to them all.

Two Important Aids
to Help You Learn How to Dance

Before going on to the actual instructions in the basic Fox Trot step, I want to impress upon you two important aids that I have devised to help you in learning not only this step, but all the dances given in this book.

1. THE MURRAY FOOTPRINTS
2. THE USE OF MUSIC

These aids have been developed in my own studio and have been thoroughly tested and proved by hundreds of thousands of experiments in teaching the art of dancing. Now you can have the benefit of these aids right in your own home. You will find that they are the nearest thing possible to personally supervised instruction in my studio.

AID NUMBER ONE—THE MURRAY FOOTPRINTS

You will find a set of paper footprints in the front of this book.

These are provided as an additional aid that will make my lessons even more real to you. With the help of these footprints you can actually reconstruct each dance-step diagram on the floor, and see exactly where each foot is to be placed.

Throughout this book, you will see all the dance steps simply indicated to you by means of footprints. You can cut them out, and lay them on the floor. Then you will be able to follow my diagrams exactly.

After you cut these footprints out, you will notice that you have one set with the word START on it—

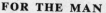

FOR THE MAN   **FOR THE GIRL**

And you also have six single footprints. (see below)

FOR THE MAN

FOR THE GIRL

Here is how these footprints can help you visualize my instructions: throughout the book you will find a number of diagrams similar to the one shown on the next page. In each case, lay the footprints out on the floor in the same pattern as the diagram.

Note: Girls will find it simpler to walk forward during this one beginning exercise, rather than try to walk backward in the normal Girl's step that they will use later.

HOW TO LAY OUT THE FOOTPRINTS

1. Place the joined footprints (labeled START) on the floor, and stand directly upon them, with your left foot on the white footprint and your right foot on the black footprint.
2. Now take a *comfortable* step in the direction of FOOTPRINT 1, as shown in the diagram, and place FOOTPRINT 1 where your foot indicates. (When I say "take a *comfortable* step," I mean take as long a step as is comfortable for you — one of twelve to fifteen inches, and one that permits you to go reasonably far without losing grace or balance.)
3. Now take a comfortable step in the direction of FOOTPRINT 2 and place the correct footprint down in that spot.
4. Proceed in like manner, and place FOOTPRINTS 3, 4, 5, and 6 in the positions indicated in the diagram.

NOW—actually try this with the diagram given here.

When you have done this, take your position on the footprints labeled START. Then step forward and put your *left* foot directly on *footprint 1.*

Now place *right* foot on *footprint 2— left* foot on *footprint 3—right* foot on *footprint 4—left* foot on *footprint 5— right* foot on *footprint 6.*

Repeat this two or three times, remembering always to step directly on the footprints, but don't become too absorbed in fitting your foot exactly to each print as though it were a shoe. The prints are intended to serve only as *guiding places* for your feet.

HOW TO PUT THESE FOOTPRINTS INTO ACTUAL USE

The footprints are, of course, only a part of this method. They help *show* you what my instructions *tell* you. Don't lead yourself astray by using only the footprints and diagrams. Remember that the *printed* instructions are the backbone of what you are learning—the pictures and diagrams are given to help you visualize the instructions.

Make your feet—rather than your head—"memorize" the motion of the steps. Constant practice will soon enable you to do each step without even thinking about it.

Learn only one dance step at a time. Take up the next only after you are sure that you have mastered the one before it.

Use the footprints for every one of the diagrams shown in this book. (Do not be misled by the apparent space between the footprints in some of the diagrams. The footprints in certain cases are spread far apart for the sake of clarity. In every instance, however, step off the correct distance yourself before placing the footprints on the floor. And again—take long, comfortable steps that suit your own stride.)

These Murray Footprints have been made a definite part of this method because I firmly believe they add a new and novel element that is certain to make learning to dance more fun than ever. They give you still more to "go by"—really a more mistake-proof method than has ever before been developed, and one which will help to make the lessons themselves really a fascinating game.

Use the footprints—get the full value of their help. If you have never danced at all up to now, you will find them indispensable. When you are thoroughly familiar with the step you are learning—then, *and only then,* pick up the footprints and practice the step without them.

REVIEW

1. Make sure that you are using the correct footprints (Man or Girl).
2. The *right* footprint is always *black* — the *left* always *white.*
3. Keep your feet together with heels touching in the starting position.
4. When you place the footprints on the floor, step off the normal distance between them — don't just lay them down by guesswork.
5. When you are practicing the steps, don't try to fit your foot *exactly* to each print—simply use them as a guide.

And now this one new thing to learn about the use of the *Murray Footprints:*

Whenever you take a step of any kind as indicated by a numbered footprint, *always place your weight on that foot.* In some cases you will find that the diagram includes a dotted footprint. This indicates an exception—*don't place your weight on a dotted footprint.*

NOTE: In many of these lessons, both the Man's part and the Girl's part are given. Use the appropriate footprints as indicated in these diagrams. However, in all lessons in the basic steps, only one set of footprints is shown in the diagram. Wherever this occurs, the Girl should use the Man's footprints. For your guidance you will find in every such instance the following note:

NOTE TO GIRLS: Use the Man's footprints in this lesson.

AID NUMBER TWO—THE USE OF MUSIC

As I told you before, a knowledge of music is not necessary to learn to dance; however, to become a good dancer, you must *practice* diligently to suitable music.

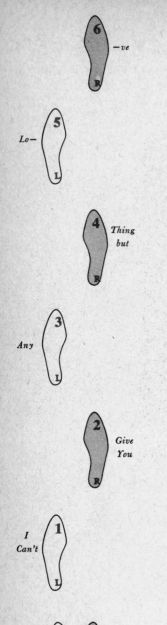

DEVELOPING RHYTHM

In each of the following lessons I have chosen a well-known melody to which I suggest you practice. If you are not familiar with the melody I've chosen, it might be advisable to get someone to sing it over for you a few times. Since in every instance I have given only the first line of the song, you should have no difficulty in learning it.

In most of the following diagrams you will note that, aside from the number given on each footprint, there is a word, or one syllable of a word, or a number of words printed alongside of it. When practicing the exercise, put the foot down on the appropriate footprint, and keep it there for the time it takes you to sing the word, or words, printed alongside of it. (See the example on this page.)

This will help you develop the proper rhythm for that particular step.

PART TWO

THE FOX TROT

The Fox Trot

WE ARE now ready to consider the Fox Trot, which is unquestionably America's most popular dance. Ninety per cent of all our popular songs are written to Fox Trot rhythm. When danced by two experienced dancers, it is a beautiful dance that is a pleasure to watch as well as to do.

The Fox Trot may seem to be complicated, but it is actually composed of only two basic steps that are skillfully blended and combined to make a fascinating and ever-varying pattern. When you have thoroughly mastered these two basic elements you will find that all the many possible variations are comparatively simple to learn. These two basic steps are:

1. THE WALKING STEP (forward and backward)
2. THE CHASSÉ (or side step)

I am going to take up these steps in great detail so that you will be able to understand them thoroughly. I want you to spend an unusually great amount of time and practice on the Fox Trot because it, more than any other single dance, is the foundation for almost all the clever modern dances that are in vogue today.

THE FOX TROT WALKING STEP

ALL THE thought and care that you have already put into learning the previous One Step are now going to be applied to the walking step as it is used in the Fox Trot.

Actually this step is the same as the One Step you have just learned, but with two important exceptions:

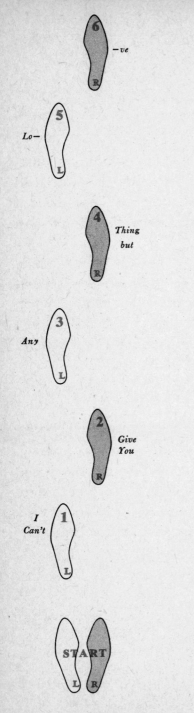

1. The Fox Trot walking step is taken to *two* beats of the music instead of only one as was the case in the One Step.

2. You will rise up on your toes at every step, and sink down on the flat of your foot as you put your weight on it. This gives life and zest to your walk.

Generally the step is *long* and the walk is rather *slow*.

Now arrange the footprints on the floor in accordance with the diagram.

Here is how the step is taken to every *two* beats of the music:

1. Place your whole foot forward flat on the floor at the *first* beat.

2. Rise up slowly on your toes at the *second* beat.

How the Fox Trot Walking Step Is Danced

PRACTICE

Take your position at START with heels together.

1. Simply step forward with the left foot flat on the floor, and rise slightly on your toes.
2. Bring the right foot forward and rise on it.
3. Keep going forward (in the Line of Direction as explained on page 18), right hand to the wall. At first exaggerate the rising and falling movement on the toes in order to bring the foot muscles properly into action.
4. After you have tried this for several times only as a walk, then begin to practice the step, singing aloud the words of "I Can't Give You Anything But Love," and walk in time to the words printed alongside each foot on the diagram. They will indicate how to take the step to every two beats of the music.

Always keep these general characteristics in mind while practicing the Fox Trot Walking Step.

1. It is taken to two beats of the music.
   First beat—foot forward flat on the floor.
   Second beat—rise up on your toes.
2. The steps are long and slow.
   Give a full second to each step.
3. Rise and fall as you walk.
   Don't be afraid to exaggerate the rising and falling motion a trifle while you are learning. When you know the step well enough to try it with a partner, you can modify the rising motion until it is hardly noticeable and you won't even have to think about it then.

−ve

Lo−

Thing
but

Any

Now practice the Walking Step around
the room as shown in this diagram.

Give
You

I
Can't

START

39

THE CHASSÉ

THE CHASSÉ is merely a step taken to the side instead of forward. It is done in the same manner as the Walking Step. Here is how to do it:

Take your position at START with your heels together.

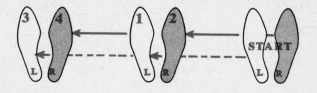

1. Step to the left with your left foot.
2. Draw your right foot up to your left.
3. Continue taking steps to the side, taking each step to every *two* beats of the music.

NOTE: The Chassé can be done either to the left (as above) or to the right.

GIRLS: Use the Man's footprints in this lesson.

Why You Should Learn to Dance Alone at First

Don't worry for a minute about the mistaken idea that it is "impossible" to learn to dance without a partner. Too many thousands of my pupils have already learned to become excellent dancers by themselves to let the thought even bother you.

In fact, by practicing alone at first you will develop a surer sense of poise and balance than you would ever acquire by being draped on a partner!

And until you do learn to dance properly alone, it is not only unwise but really an imposition to ask anyone to dance with you.

Now That You're
Ready for a Partner

UP TO NOW, you have been dancing alone. You have learned to keep time with the music, and to dance the One Step and the Fox Trot. But you aren't practicing the exercises in this book in order to dance by yourself! What you want, of course, is to dance with a *partner*. And now the moment has arrived.

What is the difference between dancing alone and dancing with a partner? Aside from the obvious fact that you are holding, and being held by, someone else, *there is no basic difference.* You take the same steps. You follow the rhythm of the music in the same way. In fact, you do everything exactly as you have learned it thus far; there is nothing for you to change in any way at all.

Therefore, dancing with a partner is simply the next step in your progress. There is no reason for you to be timid about it. For the sake of your own self-confidence it might be well, of course, before dancing in public, to practice in private with someone you know well. Or if this cannot be arranged conveniently, then to try out your dancing first when you are with a small group, rather than on a crowded dance floor.

In either case, you have come to a milepost in your dancing career! From now on, you are ready for all the fun and all the enjoyment that good dancers share when they have music in their feet and the joy of dancing in their hearts. Now you are really ready to *dance!*

How to Hold Your Partner

There is nothing mysterious about "how to hold your partner" in dancing. Your position should be guided by comfort, common sense and convention—and that is all there is to it.

Outside a few eccentric crazes like the Bunny Hug, Charleston, Black Bottom and so on, position in ballroom dancing hasn't changed appreciably in the past thirty years.

Youngsters have always had fads in their dancing style. One year you may find young girls leaving their right arms outstretched, palms up—as though feeling for raindrops. By the next season they will have forgotten that fad and will adopt another distinctive style.

Some youngsters assume exaggerated dancing positions merely to cover their embarrassment at not knowing what to do. As their dancing improves, they will drop affectations. Young people are more comfortable when they dance exactly as their friends do—wise parents realize this and overlook short-lived styles.

In this book we are concerned only with presenting to you the quickest and easiest means of becoming a good dancer—popular with all partners. A correct dancing position will help to make this possible.

Ten rules for a correct dancing position:

1. You can practice correct dancing position very easily in your own room, without a partner. Face a mirror and stand erect. Don't strain—simply stand naturally and comfortably as though you were about to walk down the street. Now rise so that your weight is placed evenly on the soles of your shoes—no weight on your heels. Hum a popular tune and walk about in time to the rhythm until you feel fully at ease.

2. You will find it helpful to raise your arms in typical dancing position as you practice alone. Do not hold your elbows unnaturally high—it is tiring, unnecessary and out of date.

Glance in the mirror and you will see that a medium elbow height forms the most graceful line.

3. Looking at yourself standing erect, with your arms up, will remind you to hold yourself tall. Good dancing posture is flattering. It will help you to form the habit of holding your head high, with your chest out and chin in. Bring out the best in your looks!

4. Keep your heels off the floor as much as possible. A flat-footed, firm stance belongs on the golf course—not on the dance floor. Keeping your weight over the soles of your feet will make you feel quicker and lighter as a partner.

5. Keep your feet close together, unless you are taking a definite step to the side. This is one of the most important things for you to remember. Without this, you can never hope to be a good dancer or to even "get by" in appearance. Walk toward your mirror in dance position; see how you look when your feet are apart. It's not a pretty sight, is it? Now, walk again and make a conscious effort to pass your feet closely together. Are you sold on why this is so important in dancing?

6. For graceful dancing, you must learn to turn your toes out, rather than in. Again, a peek at your mirror will convince you why this looks better.

7. Now is the time for you to stop worrying. You have seen yourself as others will see you, so you should feel secure and ready for teamwork with a partner. When dancing with some-

Both partners should stand comfortably erect and close enough to one another so that each step is easily followed.

The Man's right arm is correctly placed around the Girl, with his hand held just below her shoulder blade.

one, adopt the position that is most comfortable for both of you. Not so close together that you have no freedom of movement—but not too far apart.

8. Do not curl your arm under your partner's. Fancy, trick holds should be put away with your high school diploma.

9. A man leads best when he holds his partner in front of him or an inch or so to his right.

10. Don't lean forward or backward—just assume a natural, comfortable position and your partner will find you a natural, comfortable dancing companion.

Don't hold your elbows unnaturally high.

Don't stand too far apart.

Don't be too wrapped up in each other.

Don't extend your arm too rigidly.

HINTS FOR THE MAN

1. There is a logical reason for a Man's left arm to be extended while he dances. It is held out so as to avoid collisions with other couples as you dance by. But, your arm does not have to extend as rigidly and inflexibly as a bumper—nor does your elbow have to be held at an uncomfortably sharp angle. Simply hold the Girl's hand lightly but firmly, with your left arm in an easy, graceful curve.

2. As you dance, look over the Girl's right shoulder. By holding your partner directly in front of you or a bit to your right,

47

you will have a clear view of what's ahead. You are the leader—so it is up to you to choose a clear path.

3. Hold your partner firmly enough to guide her. A weak, listless hold will not inspire her confidence in you. Hold your hand at a comfortable height on the middle of her back. There is no cut-and-dried rule for this.

4. Always start your first step forward with your left foot. Let your toes lead and step directly toward your partner's right foot. Don't worry, she'll be moving hers backward.

HINTS FOR THE GIRL

1. As you dance, look over your partner's right shoulder for two reasons:

a. Your feet naturally point in the same direction as your eyes. By looking ahead, you will stay in correct and comfortable alignment with your partner.

b. It may seem fascinating at first but it soon becomes an uncomfortable strain when partners gaze hypnotically at each other while dancing. Try it with a girl friend; you'll find that she looks owl-like when her face is too close to yours.

2. Always be ready to take your first step backward with your right foot. A man steps forward on his left. Give him a chance to get going.

3. Let your toes lead in every step that you take. It will lengthen your step by at least six inches. Besides, stretching out with your toes will make you look ten times better to the stag line.

4. The secret of good balance is to hold your left hand very firmly on the back of your partner's right shoulder. You will find more about this under the pointers on following. Never wrap your left hand and arm around your partner's neck. It won't add glamour—it will simply pull you off balance.

THE CURVE OF LEARNING

College professors have a useful phrase to describe a student's progress. They call it the "curve of learning." When it is put down on paper, it usually looks about like this:

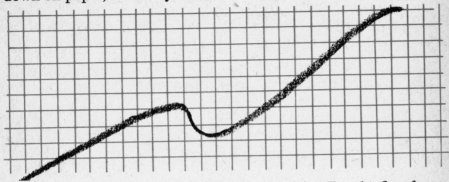

The average student starts out in high spirits. For the first few lessons his confidence keeps mounting. He forges ahead quickly —he feels sure that *he* will learn all there is to know in just another lesson or two! But in his enthusiasm he may try to bite off more than he can chew. Then oops!—the curve may go into a nose dive. And the student may have a temporary case of being "in the dumps."

Once this point is passed, however, there shouldn't be any trouble. Progress from here on is usually steady. Even if it should happen that at some particular stage of these lessons you suddenly feel like saying, "I'll never learn to dance—I might just as well give it up," don't be discouraged. You are probably then just about to begin to see the light. You are reaching the stage of *understanding,* and from then on your progress should be rapid.

Don't worry if you have a few "ups and downs" in learning to dance. Far from being signs of hopelessness, they are a natural, normal, healthy part of the learning process. Remember the curve of learning—*expect* to learn more quickly some days than others—don't try to learn everything all at once—and *be sure* your feet *"know"* each lesson before going on to the next.

The Secrets of Leading

THE DANCE FLOOR is the one place where the weaker sex prefers to remain submissive. Girls expect their partners to set the pace— to choose and direct the steps. All that they ask of you is a definite indication of where you are heading.

To give this definite indication, a man must first be clearly certain of just what he does want to do. If he is not sure of himself, how can he expect a partner to be able to follow him? There is no short-cut to good leading. It takes a definite, well-defined knowledge of the steps.

So, the one and only rule is: know the steps! Then you will move with assurance and your partners will feel a glow of pride and confidence in your ability.

Believe it or not, a girl does not need to be pushed, pulled or hauled to make her go your way. When you can do your own part well, you won't have to worry about leading. Reserve your strong-arm tactics for other times, other places than the dance floor.

Sometimes, when dancing with a brand-new partner who can follow but is not yet familiar with your style of dancing, you may have to do a bit of guiding. This is done with your right hand

and arm. Always hold your right hand firmly just above your partner's waist—you will find that she will respond easily to a light pressure. Your left hand does very little toward leading.

POINTERS FOR GOOD LEADERS

1. When dancing with a new partner for the first time, start off with very simple steps. You then become acquainted with each other's style in dancing.

2. Most good dancers lead the same step at least twice in succession. It makes their dancing more flowing—and it gives them time to plan a graceful sequence to their pattern of steps. It is far better to do the same step several times than rush into quick, jerky changes.

3. Don't be afraid to pause, in position with your partner, at the beginning of each dance. Listen to the music, make sure of your timing and then start forward, sure and confident of yourself.

4. Never count for your partner unless you don't care what she thinks of you. Neither is it necessary for you to tell her, in words, what you expect to do next. Knowing your own part well and holding your right hand firmly on her back will convey a sufficient message to her.

WHICH IS A RIGHT TURN, AND WHICH IS A LEFT?

This is a question that sometimes is a little confusing to a beginner. To help you recognize the two turns quickly, here are two aids to turning in the proper direction:

This Is a Right Turn

To make a right turn, look over your right shoulder and let the rest of your body follow.

To make a right turn, move the left hand forward.

—and This Is a Left

To make a left turn, look over your left shoulder and let the rest of your body follow.

To make a left turn, move the left hand backward.

How Learning to Lead Will Help a Girl's Dancing

If you are like most girls and women, you will be shocked when you read this—To be a better dancer, learn to lead.

But, here's a simple test that may help to convince you. Think back to the girls you knew at school. Select those girls who were in demand at every dance—the girls who had plenty of "cut-ins," who were never wallflowers. Now, think it over, weren't they the ones who could lead the other girls as partners?

I first hit upon this theory many years ago. The idea of teaching girls to lead was completely contrary to the accepted beliefs of the day. However, I was sure of the logic and common sense in back of my theory, and I decided to try it out.

I visited classes that we held in girls' clubs, schools and colleges. I asked the members of each group to vote for the best dancers among their girl friends. Without a single exception, every good dancer who was selected was a girl who could lead!

Frankly, it has taken a great deal of courage to uphold my strong convictions. Most women cling tenaciously to the belief that "leading will ruin a girl's dancing." It usually takes me a long time to convince mothers that their daughters can become popular dancing partners more quickly by first learning to lead other girls.

The Arthur Murray girl teachers are noted for their ability to follow any partner. The first step in the training is to learn to lead all partners in all dances. In our studios we now teach all girl pupils to lead before teaching them to follow.

Two Reasons Why Learning to Lead Will Make a Girl a Better Dancer

1. Have you ever skated hand-in-hand? If so, you know that it is only fun when you and your partner strike out and glide at the

same moment. If one of you is slower and misses the rhythm, twosome skating becomes boring and uncomfortable.

Dancing with a partner works on the same principle. A girl must dance *with* her partner—not *after* him. She must express herself in time with the music, not wait woodenly and lifelessly, depending on a strong push-and-pull lead. A girl who can lead understands the music and she can step out rhythmically, at the exact same time as her partner. Any man will enjoy her dancing because it feels alert, alive, vital.

2. Once a girl can lead, she begins to realize and appreciate the man's part. She discovers what she is expected to do when she is following a partner. A girl who can lead the man's part in any step, will be able to follow that step twice as lightly and twice as well. To dance with true poise and assurance, you need the confidence that knowledge brings. Learn to lead each step first, then you'll follow it easily.

There are two important points to remember about girls learning to lead:

1. When dancing with other girls, don't lead more than half the time. Take equal turns leading and following. Don't let yourself be forced into leading all the time, just because you happen to be a good leader.
2. Don't get into a rut by leading only a few steps. Learn to lead as many steps as you know how to follow.

To dance with true poise and assurance, the Girl will be wise to learn the Man's part of each step even before attempting to do her own part.

And last but by no means least, learning to lead also helps her to develop perfect posture—the result of a thorough understanding of every part of dancing.

The Secret of Following

I ONCE met a girl who was very unhappy. She said to me: "I don't understand it, Mr. Murray; boys never cut in on me but I know I can dance—why, I can follow anyone." I danced with her and found that she could follow, provided that I led her in the few simple steps with which she was familiar. As soon as I attempted anything more advanced, she was at a complete loss.

I asked her: "Do most of your partners do these same steps I've been doing with you?"

"Why, yes," she said. "That's exactly the way they dance."

So I explained that her partners were held down. They could do only those few steps because those were all she could follow. I showed her that I could not lead her in any of my other steps without having her falter or stumble.

That girl is only one of the many girls and women who believe that they can follow anyone, and then they wonder why they are not in demand as partners.

A man is limited in his dancing to what his partner can do. He finds it dull and uninteresting when he is hampered in his choice of steps by his partner's lack of knowledge. Here is a list of pointers that will help you to become a popular dancer, sought after over and over again.

TEN RULES FOR FOLLOWING

1. Know the basic steps and their possible combinations. Isn't it logical that you cannot dance well with a man until you are familiar with the steps he will do?

2. Give your partner a feeling of freedom in his forward steps —keep your feet out of his way. You can develop a long, free, swinging backward step. Try it: Step back as far as possible,

toes leading. Keep your foot off the floor until you step with your weight on it. Exaggerate by lifting your feet high off the floor as you practice.

3. Let your toes lead. Look at your foot when you take a plain walking step. Now watch what happens when you stretch with your toes. It is a simple matter of arithmetic; you can add actual inches to your step merely by pointing your toes. Practice a long, graceful stride backward, forward and to each side, letting your big toe point the way.

4. Dance on your toes—it will help to make you lighter.

5. Be ready for the next step. Don't slide your feet along the floor, lift and pass them through the air instead. Invest in practicing this . . . it pays big dividends in popularity with partners.

6. Do not make your steps too short. A short step may seem dainty to you but it will spell disaster to your dancing. Prove this to yourself by leading one of your girl friends. Tell her to take short steps—it will convince you immediately why you need to develop a long dancing stride.

7. To follow well, you must relax, of course, but do you know the true meaning of the word "relax"? It does *not* mean letting your body sag and making your partner carry your whole weight. You must first limber up your muscles so that they respond to whatever dancing steps your partner may do.

8. The opposite of complete relaxation is "tenseness." But, you cannot cure a stiff, tense body by commanding it to relax. Tenseness comes from a feeling of insecurity and from a lack of training. Learning the steps will give you security and confidence . . . practicing the "Exercises" in this book will give you training. Don't envy popular girls—rival them!

9. You must have good balance. No girl can be a pleasure to lead until she can balance her own weight. Do not lean or bear down heavily on your partner; he has to hold his own arms up throughout the entire dance. Simply hold firmly with your left

hand in back of your partner's right shoulder. Hold on very firmly—he won't feel your weight.

10. Learn your steps and train your muscles on your own time. Then you will be automatically limber and ready to follow a partner without a thought of your feet or your steps. He's the leader; don't be ahead of him or drag after him—just dance *with* him.

How Is the Girl to Know
What Her Partner Is Going to Do Next?

To a girl who has never danced with a partner, this is perhaps the most mystifying question of all!

The simple answer is, that if she has learned her part of the *steps*, she will know instinctively "what comes next." Even though her partner tries many variations of steps, she will follow him readily if—through practice—she has already developed a proper sense of dance rhythm.

For a dance has rhythm just as a musical composition has. And a good dancing partner will no more destroy that rhythm with an awkward or out-of-place step than an orchestra leader would interrupt a mellow serenade with a discordant note from a blaring trombone!

CORRECT POSITION OF FEET

All dancing is made up of combinations of the five correct positions of the feet shown on this spread. They're simple. They're natural. But they are tremendously important, because they are the actual "foundation" of all your dancing.

Study each of these pictures closely. Read the directions until you know them by heart. Then get that knowledge down into your feet. Practice these five positions over and over. Make them second nature to you, and you will be grateful for the rest of your dancing life.

Well-trained, smartly-turned feet are the mark of a good dancer. The timid, dull, unskilled dancer shuffles along any old way. The interesting dancer has feet so filled with lively, controlled grace that they virtually *sparkle!*

1. When starting to dance, or when the step brings your feet together, this is the correct position for them.

2. When your feet are apart, the toes are always turned out and your weight should rest on one foot only.

3. In bringing your feet together again, you may vary the
position shown in the first
picture by placing the heel of
one foot at the instep of the
other.

4. Walking forward or backward should always be in a
straight "chalk line"—placing one foot directly in front
(or back) of the other.

5. The toes of one foot placed
at the heel of the other foot
produces this pleasing variation of the position shown in
the third picture.

The Magic Step

AFTER 30 years of teaching, I hit upon a discovery that changed our entire system of teaching. I found that *one* easy step was the basis for seventy-five percent of all existing Fox Trot steps. We call it the Magic Step, because it can be done in twenty-seven different ways.

Before I discovered the Magic Step, all variations of the Fox Trot had to be learned separately. All combinations had different counts and it was necessary for a pupil actually to memorize a great many steps which seemed unrelated to one another.

But now, with the Magic Step, you really learn a pattern. This pattern is based on two slow and two quick steps, and it quickly becomes as automatic as walking. The music itself seems to guide you without your thinking: "What shall I do next?"

MAN'S PART
READD UP

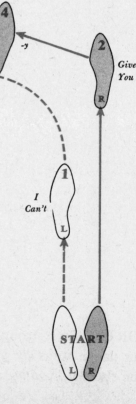

4. Draw right foot up to left quickly, weight on right.

3. Quick chassé—or side step —to left.

2. Slow walking step forward, right foot.

1. Slow walking step forward, left foot.

START

Note that the first two steps are done slowly and the last two steps quickly.

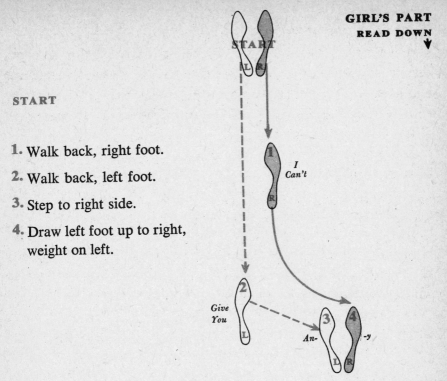

START

1. Walk back, right foot.

2. Walk back, left foot.

3. Step to right side.

4. Draw left foot up to right, weight on left.

This combination consists of two walking steps backward, followed by a quick chassé—or side step—to right.

Note that the first two steps are taken slowly, the last two steps quickly.

For further details, read the Man's part.

IMPORTANT: I strongly recommend that you learn the following dance steps *by yourself.* Don't try dancing them with anyone else *until you are sure that you know your own part first.*

61

The Conversation Step

THIS IS another popular variation of the Magic Rhythm step and is danced to Fox Trot music. In the "Conversation" position, shown here, the man may drop his left hand and the girl her right, and both dance forward, side by side, talking the while.

The Man begins with his left foot.

MAN'S PART

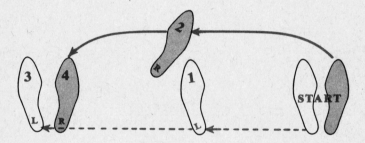

START

1. Slowly step sidewise to left.

2. Slowly cross right foot in front of left.

3. Quick chassé to left.

4. Bring right foot up to left.

Note that the first two steps are taken slowly; the last two quickly.

The Girl's steps are taken with her right foot, sideways.

GIRL'S PART

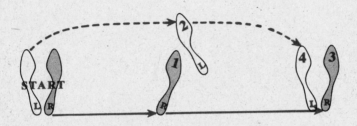

START

1. Slowly step sidewise to right.

2. Cross left foot in front of right.

3. Quick chassé to right.

4. Quickly draw left foot up to right, heels together.

The Girl's part is just the opposite of the Man's. All of her steps are taken sideward to the right. As the Man starts with his left foot, the Girl naturally must start with her right. If you will learn the Man's part first, you will find your own part very easy to do!

THE CONVERSATION STEP—OPEN POSITION

3.

4.

When dancing with a partner, the Conversation Step may be done in a half-open position as illustrated above. This step allows partners to talk and dance easily.

The Swing Step

THE SWING STEP is a popular variation of the Magic Step.

MAN'S PART

Any

Give You

I   *Can't*

START

START

1. Side step to left.

2. Draw right foot up to left.

3. Side step to left—pause for
   a half second with weight
   on left.

4. Swing right foot up to left
   (no weight on right).

5. Step to right side on right.

6. Swing left foot up to right
   (no weight on left).

Note particularly that no weight is placed on the right foot in fourth step; and no weight is placed on left foot in sixth step. This swinging movement gives this step its charm.

GIRL'S PART

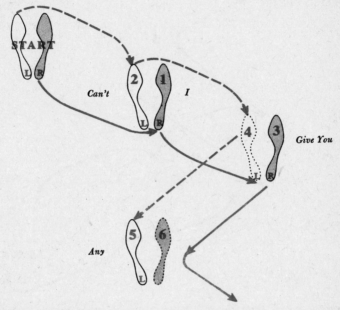

START

1. Side step to right.

2. Draw left foot up to right.

3. Side step to right—pause for a half second with weight on right foot.

4. Swing left foot up to right (no weight on left).

5. Step to left side on left foot.

6. Swing right foot up to left (no weight on right).

The Magic Right Turn

**MAN'S PART
READ UP**

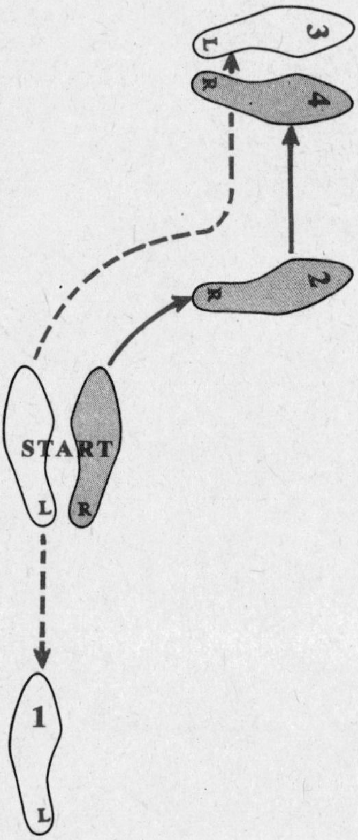

4. Bring the right foot up to the left, count four.

3. Now place the left foot about twelve inches to the left side, count three.

2. For the second count, step forward on your right foot, turning to right.

1. On the first count step straight back on the left foot, placing your entire weight on that left foot.

START

NOTE: *(Man)* As you step forward on your right foot you turn to the right.

(Girl) As you step back on your left foot you turn to the left.

The Magic Left Turn

START

1. On the first count step forward on left foot, turning left. Place your entire weight on that left foot.

2. For second count, step back on your right foot.

3. Now place the left foot about twelve inches to the left side, count three.

4. Bring right foot up to left, count four.

NOTE TO GIRLS: Use the Man's footprints in this lesson.

The Senior Walk

THIS COMBINES a forward and backward magic step to make an interesting variation.

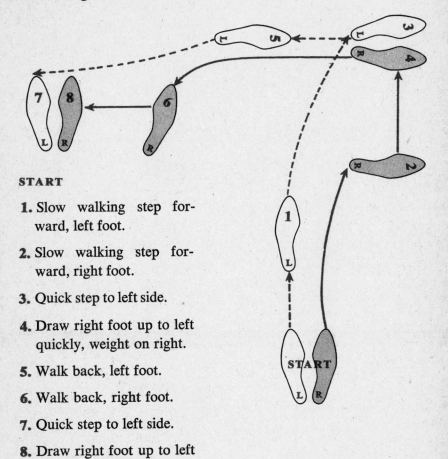

START

1. Slow walking step forward, left foot.

2. Slow walking step forward, right foot.

3. Quick step to left side.

4. Draw right foot up to left quickly, weight on right.

5. Walk back, left foot.

6. Walk back, right foot.

7. Quick step to left side.

8. Draw right foot up to left quickly, weight on right.

The Girl's part is just the opposite of the Man's—she starts backward with her right foot.

The Triple Chassé with Corté

MAN'S PART

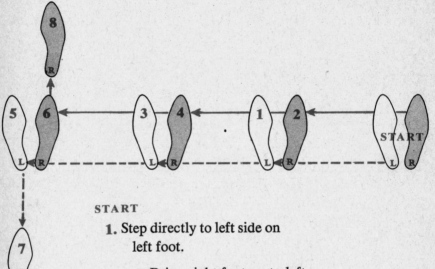

START

1. Step directly to left side on
   left foot.

2. Bring right foot up to left,
   weight on right. Repeat
   for **3, 4, 5** and **6.**

7. Step straight back on left,
   bending left knee slightly.

8. Step   straight   forward
   right.

Note: The first six steps are done quickly, the last two are taken
slowly.

GIRL'S PART

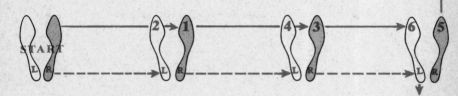

START

1. Step with right foot to
   right.

2. Draw left foot up to right,
   weight on left. Repeat for
   3, 4, 5 and 6.

7. Step straight forward on
   right, bending right knee
   slightly.

8. Step straight back on left.

The Girl's part is just the opposite of the Man's. With the right foot take three chassés to the right, dipping after the third.

The Forward Magic Rhythm

ONE OF the most graceful variations of the Magic Step is the Forward Magic Rhythm. It has always been extremely popular among the better dancers because it allows the dancer to move rapidly and gracefully across the floor. The charm of the step for the beginner is that it is very easy to learn.

The Forward Magic Rhythm is made up of two slow steps and two quick steps taken forward. The first two steps are slow, the last two are short and quick.

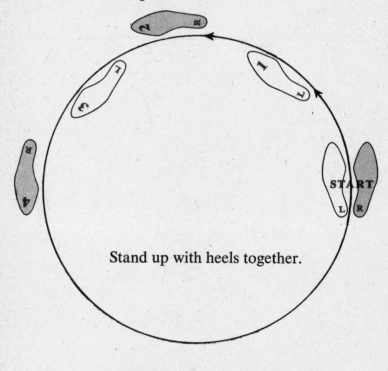

Stand up with heels together.

START

1. Take a long step forward on left.

2. A long step forward on right foot.

3. Step forward on left.

4. Step forward on right.

74

That's all. Just two long, slow steps, and two short, quick steps.

All four steps in the Forward Magic Rhythm should be done very smoothly.

Be sure that you do not let your heels touch the floor when doing the *last two quick steps*.

The Forward Magic Rhythm is one of the most useful dance steps for weaving in and out on a crowded floor.

Now practice this graceful step, following the chorus and the Magic Rhythm.

The Girl's part of the Forward Magic Rhythm is just the opposite of the Man's. It is very important to let your toes lead, as you dance backward.

A Simple Fox Trot Routine

HAVE YOU ever noticed a good swimmer who is thoroughly at home in the water? He dives in . . . swims the crawl for a few strokes . . . turns over on his back, and floats a while . . . then continues with the trudgen or breast stroke. Perhaps he treads water or swims lazily on his back. He varies the strokes at his command as the mood seizes him.

So it is with a good dancer. Master of the basic steps and their variations, he weaves his own patterns upon the dance floor guided by the mood of the music or his own whim. His dancing is interesting to his partner and an endless joy to himself.

Therefore, when I give you a simple Fox Trot routine, as I do here, remember it is merely *one* suggested way to combine the steps you have learned. *Make your own combinations*. Only when the dance becomes your own original creation will you experience the joy of dancing to the full.

I give this routine to you for two reasons:

1. It will serve as a review of the steps you have learned. As such it is particularly valuable. Pay special attention to the *changes* from one step to another. Go from one step into the next smoothly and without halting. Remember, each step starts with the LEFT foot for the Man, and the RIGHT foot for the Girl.

2. It has been devised so it can be practiced to the chorus of any popular Fox Trot tune. Turn on the radio or phonograph, if one is handy. Since most of the popular songs are in Fox Trot rhythm the probabilities are overwhelming that the orchestra will be playing a Fox Trot. If neither radio nor phonograph is convenient, whistle, hum, or sing aloud the chorus of any of the recent popular songs, and practice the routine to that music.

Take your position, heels together. As you begin the chorus of your song start off with the left foot, and do the first step. Continue *without pause* through the routine.

PRACTICE

COMBINATION A

1. MAGIC STEP
2. CONVERSATION STEP
3. MAGIC RIGHT TURN
4. SWING STEP

COMBINATION B

1. MAGIC STEP
2. SENIOR WALK
3. MAGIC LEFT TURN

COMBINATION C

1. MAGIC STEP
2. TRIPLE CHASSÉ WITH CORTÉ
3. FORWARD MAGIC RHYTHM

How to Achieve
Perfect Carriage

MOST PEOPLE don't know how to walk. And what's more, most people don't even know how to stand properly. Any doctor will tell you so.

Dancing is the key to correct standing and walking, for one very simple reason: You can't dance well unless you first learn how to stand and walk well.

I have seen men and women shuffle into my classes so awkwardly that I have been tempted to say: "No, you are really hopeless. There can't be an ounce of grace concealed in your body."

But of course, I don't say it—for I know from experience that the very routine of dancing *brings out* good posture. In my thirty-odd years of teaching I have seen so many ugly-duckling slouchers and slumpers turn into graceful swans that no transformation can ever surprise me.

Correct posture, once learned, is yours forever. A man who has once been in the army needs no uniform to display his soldier's training. You know at a glance he's an army man. And dancing, like military training, does develop correct posture.

It actually *helps build* the new and correct posture you find so hard to cultivate as you walk along the street, thinking "I *must* stand erect"—only to fall back into your old ways as soon as you stop thinking about it. But when you take up a new activity such as dancing, which constantly requires correct posture, you begin gradually to replace your old habits with new and good ones.

You cannot dance with ease and assurance until you know the secrets of standing and walking properly. Trying to look well merely by standing up straight just makes you look and feel stiff. Therefore, right now, it will be very helpful to you to learn the secret of correct posture.

ELEVEN KEYS TO CORRECT POSTURE

1. Dance as though your body were floating through air.

2. Dance "in the air," not close to the floor.

3. Do not sway the upper part of the body from the hips.

4. Keep your head and shoulders up.

5. Avoid deep dips and brusque or sudden motions.

6. Remember that rising too high on your toes will make you look and feel tense.

7. Above all things, be natural.

8. Do not bend your knees any more in dancing than you do in walking.

9. Never allow your feet to remain apart.

10. Pumping your arms or flouncing your elbows betrays an unconscious attempt to keep time to the music with the upper part of your body. And it shows that your feet have been improperly trained.

11. Don't drag along—or slide—or scrape or hug the floor.

Don'ts for Beginners

1. DON'T think the whole world is watching you when you step out on a dance floor. Realize that the others are either good dancers, who are having too good a time themselves to pay much attention to what you do—or that they're just fair-to-middling dancers, who are too busy taking care of their own feet to keep their eyes on any other particular couple.

2. Don't be the first couple on the floor—unless you are very sure of your dancing. Wait until the floor is comfortably filled—then step out. Until you have complete confidence in your ability, there's more safety in numbers.

3. Don't be afraid to hold your partner firmly. She won't bite you. But don't crush her with the grip of a boa constrictor, either. The correct amount of pressure for your hand while dancing, is just about the same as it would be if you were holding the Girl's arm to escort her across a street.

4. Don't worry, if you're the leader, about how you will get in step with the music. All good dancers pause, in dance position, at the beginning. They listen to the tempo before they start. There is no law that says you must start with the very first note that the orchestra plays. Listen first. Remember that the distinctive rhythm of each type of music repeats itself every three or four seconds. You're bound to hear it.

5. Don't forget that when a man takes a girl to a dance, he *always* has the first dance with her. And that it is customary, as well, to dance the last dance of the evening together. How many dances you share between these is up to the two of you—though it is exceedingly impolite for a man to monopolize a girl for the whole evening. Unless, of course, just the two are dining and dancing together at a club or hotel, with no other friends present.

The Secret of Good Balance

TO DANCE with ease, poise, and confidence, you must learn to balance your body correctly. Poor dancers, who have never learned proper balance, often find dancing tiring to their muscles—and usually to some particular set of muscles. Because their dancing position has been strained, their "legs hurt" or their "arms ache."

Good balance is the ability to maintain your equilibrium easily, lightly. If you have ever noticed a small child, toddling about, you have seen that it takes time before a steady, upright walk is achieved. We learn to balance our weight through practice.

Before we go on, supposing you try this simple balance test. Place your weight on the toes of one foot, raising the other foot off the floor for several inches, either forward or backward. Do you feel steady? Most people cannot hold this pose for more than a few seconds without wavering.

But, good balance is easy to acquire. In dancing, there are just two things necessary . . . first, to strengthen the muscles of the toes which carry your weight—second, and for girls only, learn to use your left hand as ballast—to give you added support.

Both men and girls can improve their balance and strengthen their toe muscles by dancing alone and by practicing the exercises in this book. Many men feel self-confident—they are not afraid of being wallflowers because they know that they can always ask a girl to dance. But, if those men who "get by" with poor dancing could hear what their partners say about them in the powder room, they might be more anxious to improve their technique.

Strengthening the toe muscles will serve you well in other fields than dancing. Good balance is required for football, basketball, tennis, skating, boxing, track and golf. Further, good balance gives you an attractive and a tireless walking posture.

THE BALANCE TEST FOR GIRLS

Try the "balance test" again; placing your weight on the toes of one foot, with the other foot extended in air. Now place your left hand on the top of your dresser or on the back of a chair. It's easy to stand steadily now, isn't it?

When you dance, train yourself to hold your left hand very firmly on the back of your partner's shoulder. Don't be afraid, you will not seem heavy. He will not feel the slightest discomfort from that pressure. Instead, you will seem lighter to him. If you would like to prove this to yourself, lead one of your girl friends. Have her hold on to your shoulder, steadying her full weight with her left hand. You will find that you can lead her easily, even if she drops her right arm completely.

This is the first bit of training that I give to every girl teacher in our studios. My experience has been that I must repeat this warning several times to each girl:—Hold your left hand firmly on the back of your partner's right shoulder!

PART THREE

THE WALTZ AND ITS VARIATIONS

The Waltz

FEW MODERN dances can boast of a background so rich in tradition as the Waltz. Originating in Italy four centuries ago as a round dance called the *Volte,* it has passed through many stages. Each succeeding decade has added something to its charm—until today it is recognized as one of the most beautiful dances in the world.

Most of the Waltz melodies are dreamy and romantic. The steps are smooth and gliding—the pattern of the dance is gay and joyful. And because the Waltz steps are basic—so much the foundation for many other dances—it will pay you to learn to Waltz well. The good Waltzer is generally an all-around good dancer.

Waltz Rhythm

There are *three* beats to each measure of Waltz music, and the music itself plainly suggests that you count:

ONE, two, three . . . ONE, two, three . . .

This same beat is carried through the entire Waltz, and therefore it is very easy to keep time to, once you have learned the steps.

Naturally, in every Waltz song there are both long notes and short notes; frequently one note lasts three beats, as in the familiar "Sidewalks of New York" ("East Side, West Side, All Around the Town"), in which each of the first four notes is given three beats:

EAST	SIDE,	WEST	SIDE
1-2-3	**1**-2-3	**1**-2-3	**1**-2-3

If you will hum "ONE, two, three—ONE, two, three" instead

of "East Side, etc.," to this well-known tune, I am sure you will quickly grasp its Waltz rhythm without a bit of difficulty.

Accent in the Waltz

An important key to a colorful dancing personality is *accent*. It is just as essential in dancing as in music or in speaking. A person who talks with a flat, unvarying voice and à "deadpan" expression is sure to sound like a bore.

A dancer who does not accent and vary his dancing isn't much fun to dance with. His leading has no life or pep. And by the same token, the Girl who hasn't learned to dance alone—with a full knowledge of the Man's part of each step—usually has little life to her dancing. She doesn't know how or when to accent the beat and rhythm of the dance—to express that extra something that makes dancing with her a real joy.

Dancers should emphasize, or accent, the same beat of music that the orchestra accents most. As I told you in a previous chapter, observe (or listen to, on the radio or phonograph) the accented beats of the bass drummer. When he is playing a Waltz, for example, he strikes the pedal of his drum in groups of three beats, but he strikes hardest on the first beat.

Therefore, when you practice the Waltz, you should do likewise—accent the *first* of every three steps.

And remember: Accent or emphasis is marked by the Man's left foot, and the Girl's right foot.

Try this way of injecting more life and pep into your dancing, and after only a few hours of practice you will find yourself accenting the correct beats quite naturally.

One more important point I would like to emphasize to you now is what I call the "Law of Opposites." When you step *forward* with either foot, the *opposite* shoulder is brought slightly *forward*. When you step *backward* with either foot, the *opposite* shoulder is similarly brought slightly *backward*. Make this a definite rule in your dancing.

And now for the next step in your progress toward becoming a genuinely good dancer!

How to Learn the Waltz

Even if you have danced the Waltz before, or have had any previous experience in this dance, study the following pages to be sure that you are doing it correctly.

Don't content yourself merely with memorizing the steps—you must really *know how to do* them. Each movement should be practiced over and over again until you can do it rapidly without having to think about what your feet must do. When you are dancing to fast Waltz music with a partner and have to change from one direction to another, you will be too busy to think about working out the steps.

The Waltz consists of:
1. Forward Waltz movement.
2. Backward Waltz movement.
3. Left (reverse) Waltz turn.
4. Right Waltz turn.
5. The Balance Steps.
6. The Biltmore.
7. The Yale Waltz.

These seven steps virtually comprise the Waltz as it is danced today.

The Basic Waltz Step

THE BASIC Waltz Step is composed of three simple steps. It is one of the most important steps in dancing, since this Basic Waltz Step is used for left and right turns in both the Waltz and Fox Trot. All variations in the Waltz are based on this step.

First, take the footprints and arrange them on the floor in accordance with the diagram given below.

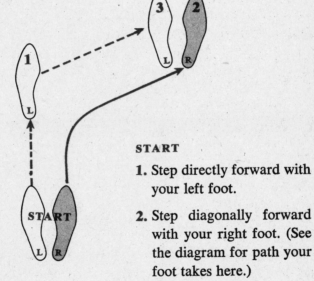

MAN'S PART
READ UP

START

1. Step directly forward with your left foot.

2. Step diagonally forward with your right foot. (See the diagram for path your foot takes here.)

3. Draw your left foot up to your right, and raise your right foot from the floor.

Each time you take a step, place your weight on it.

The Forward Waltz Step

Now ADD footprints 4, 5, and 6 to your diagram on the floor. Go back to START.

MAN'S PART
READ UP
↑

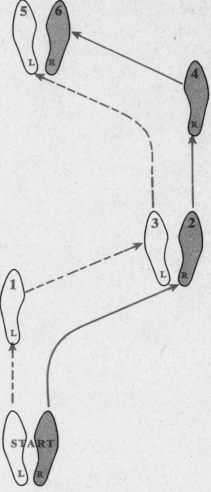

START

1. Step directly forward with your left foot.

2. Step diagonally forward with your right foot as shown in the diagram.

3. Draw your left foot up to your right, and raise your right foot from the floor.

4. Step directly forward with your right foot.

5. Step diagonally forward with your left foot as shown in the diagram.

6. Draw your right foot up to your left, and raise your left from the floor.

Each time you take a step, place your weight on it.

Now practice this step to Waltz rhythm or tempo, using the first line of the well known folk song, "The Daring Young Man on the Flying Trapeze"—the opening words of the chorus of which are, "HE - - floats through the air with the greatest of ease."

Follow the diagram—make your feet keep time to your singing. Practice makes perfect!

Repeat this step until it becomes second nature to you; until you know the step with your *feet*—not alone with your brain.

When you have mastered it, pick up the footprints, and continue the same step around the room. Sing aloud, and make your steps keep time to the words, as follows:

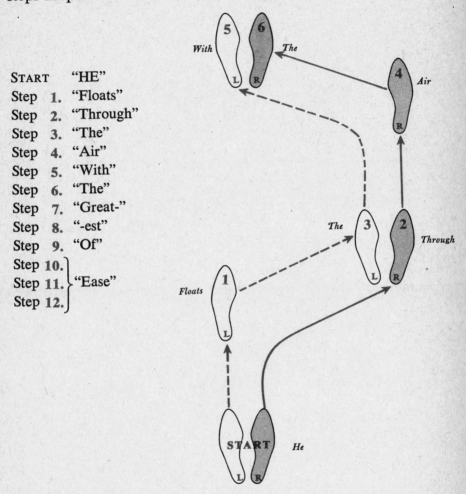

START	"HE"
Step 1.	"Floats"
Step 2.	"Through"
Step 3.	"The"
Step 4.	"Air"
Step 5.	"With"
Step 6.	"The"
Step 7.	"Great-"
Step 8.	"-est"
Step 9.	"Of"
Step 10.	
Step 11.	"Ease"
Step 12.	

NOTE TO GIRLS: Use the Man's footprints in this lesson.

The Backward Waltz Step

The backward Waltz steps are just the opposite of the forward Waltz steps.

MAN'S PART
READ DOWN
▼

START

1. Step backward with the left foot.

2. Step to right side and back slightly on right foot.

3. Draw the left foot up to right, weight on left.

4. Step directly backward with right foot.

5. Left foot to left side and slightly back.

6. Draw right foot up to left, weight on right.

Practice the backward Waltz steps around the room. Start with the left foot backward. At first go very slowly and try to do the six steps without a mistake.

Gradually do the movement faster and faster.

Do not go any further until you have mastered the forward and backward Waltz steps.

WALTZING FORWARD AND BACKWARD

After learning to Waltz forward and backward, try waltzing in both directions, first forward, then backward.

Remember that in the Waltz the Girl's part is simply the opposite of the Man's. Begin with the left foot.

1. Do the forward Waltz movement, six counts.
2. Then waltz backward, six counts.

Repeat for ten minutes, or until you can do it rapidly, and go from the forward to the backward Waltz movement without stopping.

Each time your foot takes a step, place your weight on it!

NOTE TO GIRLS

Use the Man's footprints in learning the general pattern of this step. Then when you do your long practicing, start with your right foot first.

Girls should learn the general pattern of each of these steps by using the Man's footprints which are shown throughout this section. Then, as soon as you know exactly how the step is done, I suggest that you make one slight change before you begin the necessary long drill to get the step down to your feet.

Simply start with your *right* foot first, instead of the left as marked on the diagrams for the Man. When you dance the Waltz with a partner, you will have to begin each movement with your right foot, since the Man will, of course, start with his left foot.

When you start with your right foot first you will then have to move in the direction *opposite* to that shown in the Man's diagram. You should be used to this principle now, for it has been shown in every set of Man and Girl part diagrams given you so far.

Train your feet correctly as you practice, so your response will be automatic when you try these steps with a partner.

The Box Step
for the Left Waltz Turn

WHEN DOING the turns, you do not have time to think of your steps; you must think of your direction, and the steps must be done almost mechanically. Therefore it is essential to *master* this Box Step which acts as the basis for the turn to the left.

MAN'S PART

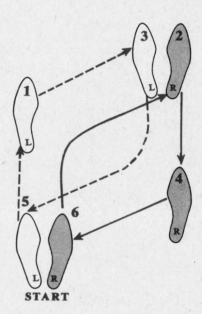

1. Step directly forward with left foot.

2. Right foot to upper right hand corner. (See diagram for path your foot takes.)

3. Close left up to right and raise right foot from floor. *This completes one Waltz step.*

4. Step straight back with right foot.

5. Left foot to the lower left-hand corner. (See diagram for path your foot takes.)

6. Close right foot up to left foot, raise left foot from the floor.

NOTE TO GIRLS: Use the Man's footprints in this lesson.

You'll notice that you end exactly where you started. Now repeat these six counts over and over until they become automatic and you don't have to think about them.

Remember to accentuate the *first* of every three steps.

The Left Waltz Turn

ARRANGE YOUR footprints on the floor in accordance with the diagram given below.

Don't place footprints too far apart!

The left turn is simply the Box Step used in turning.

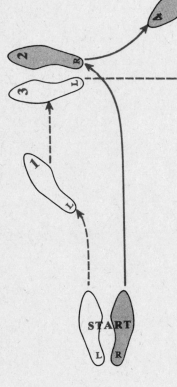

1. Step forward on left foot, turning one quarter to left.

2. Bring right foot up to right side (feet apart).

3. Close left up to right and raise right foot from floor. *This completes a quarter turn to left.*

4. Right foot back, turning one quarter to left.

5. Left foot to the side of right (feet apart), weight on left.

6. Close right up to left foot and raise left foot from floor.

Do not leave this page until you have mastered it. Spend not less than an hour in practice. If you don't understand the turn, go back to the Box Step and review.

How to Do a Complete Waltz Turn

The left Waltz turn of six counts makes only a half turn.

To do a *complete* turn, simply dance the left Waltz turn twice in succession.

In other words, do the six steps, then do the same six steps over again, without stopping.

Master perfectly the first six steps before attempting to make the complete turn of twelve counts.

If you have difficulty in learning the turn, go back and practice the Box Step for ten minutes. Remember that the left Waltz turn is merely the Box Step used in turning.

FORWARD WALTZ AND COMPLETE LEFT TURN

Begin with left foot.

PRACTICE

1. Do the forward Waltz movement, continuing straight forward for twelve counts.
2. Then do the complete left Waltz turn for twelve counts.

The Box Step

for the Left Waltz Turn

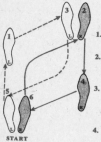

1. Step directly forward with left foot.
2. Right foot to upper right hand corner. (See diagram for path your foot takes.)
3. Close left up to right and raise right foot from floor. *This completes one Waltz step.*
4. Step straight back with right foot.
5. Left foot to the lower left-hand corner. (See diagram for path your foot takes.)
6. Close right foot up to left foot, raise left foot from the floor.

The Left Waltz Turn

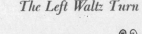

1. Step forward on left foot, turning one quarter to left.
2. Bring right foot up to right side (feet apart).
3. Close left up to right and raise right foot from floor. *This completes a quarter turn to left.*
4. Right foot back, turning one quarter to left.
5. Left foot to the side of right (feet apart), weight on left.
6. Close right up to left foot and raise left foot from floor.

94

The Box Step

for the Right Waltz Turn

LAY OUT footprints on floor in accordance with diagram below. The Box Step is the basis of the right Waltz turn.

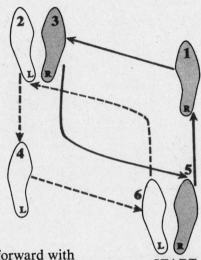

MAN'S PART

START

1. Step directly forward with the right foot.
2. Left foot diagonally across square to upper left-hand corner.
3. Draw right foot up to left, raise left foot from the floor.
4. Step directly backward with the left foot.
5. Right foot to lower right-hand corner.
6. Draw left foot up to right, raise right foot from the floor.

The Right Waltz Turn

ARRANGE YOUR footsteps on the floor in accordance with the diagram given below. Be careful to place footprints at the proper angle.

The right Waltz turn is exactly the same as the Box Step except that you turn to the right a quarter on the *first* of every three steps.

MAN'S PART

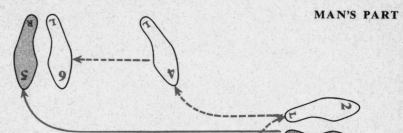

1. Step forward on right foot and at the same time turn body one quarter to right.
2. Place left foot forward to the side of right foot (feet apart).
3. Bring right foot up to left, raise left foot from floor. *This completes a quarter turn.*
4. Step directly backward with left foot, at the same time turning one quarter to right.
5. Place right foot to the side of left (feet apart).
6. Draw left foot up to right, raise right foot from floor.

You have made another quarter turn and have completed a half turn.

Go back to the beginning and do the complete step of six counts without any stops. Practice the step to music (sing aloud). Don't go on until you can put each foot down in its appropriate footprint *in time to your singing*.

NOTE TO GIRLS: Use the Man's footprints in this lesson.

FORWARD WALTZ AND RIGHT TURN COMBINATION

Begin with right foot.

1. Forward Waltz movement, six counts.
2. Right turn, six counts.
   Repeat above.

Bear in mind that you cannot learn to swim by memorizing the strokes. You learn to swim only by training the arms, legs, and body through constant *repetition,* commonly referred to as *practice*.

Have you ever tried the crawl stroke? Swimming experts say that a beginner must do it at least a thousand times before it can be mastered.

It is impossible to learn to dance by merely knowing in your mind what steps to take. You must train the muscles of your feet. This is accomplished by doing each step repeatedly until ease, poise, and confidence are acquired.

FORWARD WALTZ AND COMPLETE RIGHT TURN

Begin with right foot.

1. Do the forward Waltz movement, continuing straight forward for twelve counts.
2. Then do the complete right Waltz turn for twelve counts.

The Balance Steps

A BALANCE STEP may be taken in any direction, forward, backward or to your left or right side.

When you take a forward Balance Step, you step forward on the count of one and *hold your weight on that foot for two additional counts*. (The other foot is slowly brought up, but place no weight on it.)

BALANCE STEPS FORWARD

1. Step forward on left foot, balance weight on this foot for two additional counts. (As you step on left foot, slowly draw right foot up to left, no weight on right.)
2. Step forward on right foot, balance weight on this foot for two additional beats. (Draw left foot up to right, no weight on left.)

BALANCE STEPS BACKWARD

After you have mastered the forward Balance Steps and can do them with ease, practice the same movements progressing *backward*.

The Girl's part is exactly the same as the Man's.

BALANCE STEPS TO LEFT SIDE

Take a long step with left foot directly to left side; hold weight on left for two additional beats. (Draw right foot up to left, no weight on right.)

BALANCE STEPS TO RIGHT SIDE

Step to right side with right foot and balance weight on this foot for two additional beats of waltz music. (Draw left foot up to right, no weight on left.)

REVIEW

Have you mastered:

1. The Forward Waltz Movement?

2. The Backward Waltz Movement?

3. The Left (reverse) Waltz Turn?

4. The Right Waltz Turn?

If there is any doubt in your mind as to whether or not you have mastered the above, go back and review the steps slowly and carefully. As all the advanced Waltz variations are dependent upon the above principal movements, start at the forward Waltz movement and review every page.

The Biltmore

THIS IS a favorite step of good dancers. It consists of a slow hesitation or balance step (1, 2, 3), followed by a quick waltz (4, 5, 6).

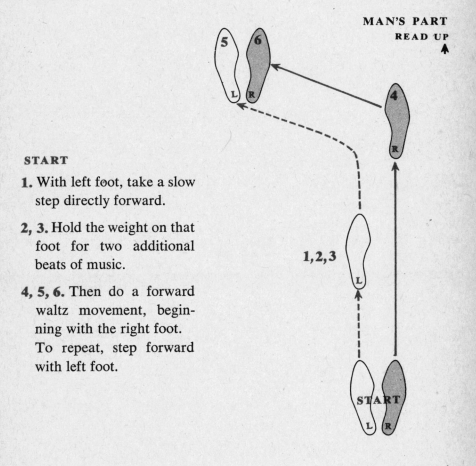

MAN'S PART
READ UP

START

1. With left foot, take a slow step directly forward.

2, 3. Hold the weight on that foot for two additional beats of music.

4, 5, 6. Then do a forward waltz movement, beginning with the right foot.
To repeat, step forward with left foot.

The Girl should learn the Man's part first. When doing her own part, she begins with the right foot and goes backward.

The Arthur Murray Turn

MAN'S PART
READ DOWN
▼

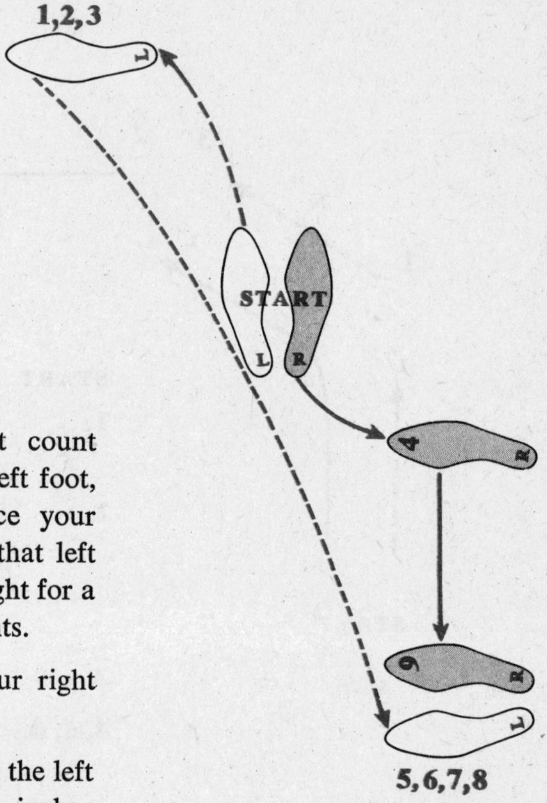

1,2,3

START

L   R

4

9

5,6,7,8

START

1, 2, 3. On the first count step forward on left foot, turning left. Place your entire weight on that left foot and hold weight for a total of three counts.

4. Step back on your right foot.

5, 6, 7, 8. Now place the left foot about twelve inches to the left side; count three.

9. Bring right foot up to left.

REPEAT THE entire step of *nine* counts.

The Yale Waltz

LIKE THE Biltmore, the popular Yale Waltz combines the forward Waltz step with the Balance Step, but in a different manner to give you an entirely new pattern.

MAN'S PART
READ UP

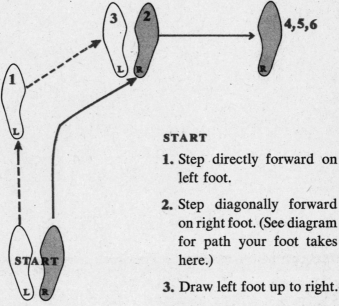

START

1. Step directly forward on left foot.

2. Step diagonally forward on right foot. (See diagram for path your foot takes here.)

3. Draw left foot up to right.

4, 5, 6. Step to right with right foot and hold weight on right for three beats of the music. Draw left up to right.

NOTE TO GIRLS: Use the Man's footprints in this lesson.

IMPORTANT: As the Waltz is the foundation of all ballroom dancing, it is urgent that the student spend not less than ten hours in practicing the Waltz steps, forward, backward, and combining these movements with the left turn and the right turn.

Modern ballroom dancing is not a cut-and-dried affair in which a series of prearranged steps or figures follow each other in any set routine. If it were, it would soon become very dull.

There is only one "must" in modern dancing—LEARN THE BASIC STEPS.

Once you have mastered these, you can combine them in an endless variety of patterns.

Therefore I say to you again and again, learn your basic steps. Practice them until you know them with your *feet*—until they become so much a part of you that you can do them without *conscious* thought. Then, and then only, can you use them to weave your own patterns. Only then will you know the real joy of the dance.

Two Simple Waltz Routines

THE WALTZ routines I have given below are not in any sense of the word to be considered final. They are merely simple combinations of the basic steps and will serve as a review of all those steps.

ROUTINE I
Start with left foot
1. Do the forward Waltz movement............Twelve counts
2. Do the complete left Waltz turn...............Twelve counts
3. Do the forward Waltz movement.................Nine counts
4. Do the complete right Waltz turn.............Twelve counts

Walk through the routine two or three times to familiarize yourself with it.

Then hum, sing, or whistle your tune, "The Man on the Flying Trapeze," and practice it to music.

ROUTINE II

Start with left foot

1. Do the forward Waltz movement...................Six counts
2. Do the half left Waltz turn...........................Six counts
3. Do the backward Waltz movement.........Twelve counts
4. Do the half left Waltz turn.............................Six counts
5. Do the forward Waltz movement...................Six counts

Walk through the routine two or three times to familiarize yourself with it.

Then hum, sing, or whistle your tune, "The Man on the Flying Trapeze," and practice it to music.

Now try these routines to the chorus of any popular Waltz tune that you know.

How to Dance Waltz Steps to Fox Trot Music

Observe closely our best dancers and you will find that they use Waltz steps to Fox Trot music at least fifty per cent of the time.

When you realize that by learning to do the Waltz steps in Fox Trot time you practically double your dancing repertoire, you can then appreciate why it will be worth your time to study this lesson slowly and carefully.

The Waltz consists of three steps. You don't have to understand music to know that a bar of Fox Trot music has four quick counts. How, then, do we fit three steps of the Waltz to four counts of Fox Trot time? Easily enough.

The first step of the Waltz is taken slowly. It is given two beats, the same as a slow walking step in the Fox Trot. The two remaining steps of the Waltz get one beat each.

Try doing the forward Waltz to Fox Trot music.

1, 2. Walk slowly forward on left foot, count one, two.
3. Step quickly to right side, three.
4. Quickly draw left foot up to right, four.

Repeat and practice the Waltz steps in time to Fox Trot music.

How to Be Graceful

THIS IS not meant for girls only. Watch a tennis player, swimmer, skater—even a boxer—and you will realize that men can be graceful, too. To be graceful means to move lightly and without effort. We are not born with this ability; it comes only through training and strengthening the muscles.

When you train to gain muscular control, your movements must be exaggerated at the start. A football player who wants to be able to kick a ball accurately, at the height of his waist, practices until he can kick as high as his head. Then the lower distance seems so easy that he can reach it with no effort at all.

Good dancers not only feel graceful to their partners but they also look graceful in motion. Study and practice these pointers—they will help you to acquire a smooth, smart dancing appearance. Remember, exaggerate at the start and you will reach perfection with ease.

1. When both feet are on the floor, try always to have them placed in one of the five standard positions as shown on pages 58 and 59.
2. Keep your heels close together in Position 1, and pass them close to each other when walking forward or backward, as in Position 4.
3. Always bring your heels together before taking a side step, as in Position 2.
4. Your feet should always work as a team, keeping as close together as the nature of the step permits. Even when the two feet are being moved in different directions, as in the figure below, notice that the correct way is to "brush" them close to one another, rather than to spread them apart at a sharp angle.
5. Lead with your toes in forward, backward, and side steps —in other words, always! Otherwise you can't dance gracefully.

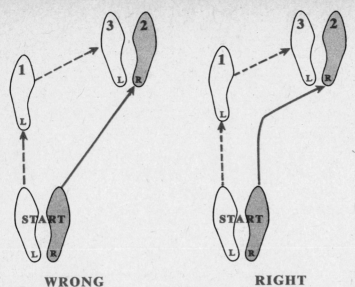

WRONG   **RIGHT**

Keep your feet close together when passing
from one step to another.

6. Keep your toes turned slightly outward.
7. Let your toes be the first to touch the floor, whether you are going forward, backward, or to the side.
8. The Girl should take the backward steps from the hip (not from the knee). There should always be a straight line from her hip to the tip of her toes.
9. Do not sway the upper part of your body independently. The upper part of the body should respond naturally and only to the motions of the feet. For example, when you step forward with your left foot, your right arm will swing forward automatically. You don't need to sway consciously from the waist.

Grace, poise, and confidence result from proper training. They are acquired gradually, and you will possess them to the full only if you make certain that you thoroughly know and are able to do all the steps that give interest and variety to your dancing.

Correct Position of Feet

I TOLD YOU before that all dancing is made up of the combination of five correct positions of feet. I am showing them to you again because they are very important. If you are ever in doubt as to what position your feet should be in, refer to this page—they MUST be in one of the positions given here.

1 When starting to dance, or when the step brings your feet together, this is the correct position for them.

2 When your feet are apart, the toes are always turned out and your weight should rest on one foot only.

3 In bringing your feet together again, you may vary the position shown in the first picture by placing the heel of one foot at the instep of the other.

4 Walking forward or backward should always be in a straight "chalk line"—placing one foot directly in front (or back) of the other.

5 The toes of one foot placed at the heel of the other foot produces this pleasing variation of the position shown in the third picture.

PART FOUR
THE LATIN AMERICAN DANCES

The Rumba

THE RUMBA, which orginated in Cuba, is unique among ballroom dances. The music has a seductive, primitive charm, and yet, when correctly danced, the Rumba is as smooth as the Fox Trot, as decorous as the Waltz.

The *one* essentially different characteristic of the Rumba is the Rumba motion. When you dance the Waltz, the Samba, the Fox Trot, you place your weight on each step that you take. But in the Rumba, *you take each step without placing your weight on that step*.

Once you learn the Rumba motion, your dancing will have a typical Cuban style. The motion is what makes the Rumba different from any other dance. It must be learned and practiced; it cannot be "faked"!

Facts About Rumba

Americans refer to all Cuban music as "Rumba." But there are more variations of tempo and style in the Rumba than in the Fox Trot. Here is a brief description of some varieties in Rumba tempo.

The very slow Rumbas are called either Bolero, Cancion Bolero or Bolero Son. The last one has a fast ending. The Danzon is of quiet, medium tempo, and the steps that fit the music are conservative in style. Then there is the Danzonette—similar to the Danzon—but the music is shorter and has more life; the Guajero—a slow to medium tempo; the Son Montuno, which is medium with a fast ending; the Guaracha, usually played very fast; and the Montuno, also fast.

The instruments used for Rumba music are distinctive and easy to recognize. The maracas are dried gourds, filled with buckshot. They are shaken like rattles and they add excitement to the music. The bongo is made of two small drums fastened together and held between the knees, drummed upon with the fingers. Finally there are the clavas, which are two pieces of hard wood, about six inches long and about an inch thick. These give a sharp, reverberating sound when struck together.

But a dancer who has mastered a pattern of steps and has practiced them in Rumba style does not have to be concerned with the names of tempos. He can fit his steps to any Rumba music. When he hears the maracas, he can dance with the true confidence that comes with knowledge.

The Secret of the Rumba Motion

It took me nine years to discover the secret of the authentic Cuban Rumba. Now that I know it, I can teach it to you in just a few minutes.

In American dances there is no hip movement. But in the Rumba there is a slight rhythmical swaying of the hips. The secret of acquiring this typical Rumba movement is in taking each step with a slightly bent knee. If this is done properly, your hips sway from side to side.

Now here is the trick of getting the Rumba motion. As you take each step with a slightly bent knee, your entire weight remains on the heel of the other foot. For instance, when you step forward with your left foot, your left knee is bent and your weight remains behind on your right foot.

The effect is just the same as walking up a flight of stairs.

The Cuban Walk

Start with your feet together. Without moving your body forward, take a short step forward with your left foot, bending your left knee . . . and as you bend your left knee, be sure that your entire weight is on the heel of your right foot. Your right foot is flat on the floor, and your right knee should be straight.

Now try it with the other foot. Take a short step forward with your right foot. The right knee should be bent, and the weight should be on the heel of the left foot and the left knee straight. When you bend your knee be sure that you do not stoop. The body is held erect.

SIDE VIEW

Start forward now, stepping as described, first left, then right.

If you hold your hands on your hips as you walk, you will notice that your weight shifts from side to side. That is the Rumba motion. That's all there is to it. You don't have to swing your hips or move any other part of your body consciously.

Now practice to the music.

Move forward left—move forward right.

Left, right, left, right.

The Rumba motion will give an authentic Cuban style to your dancing. Learning this motion does take time, but once you get it, you will use the same motion in all Rumba variations.

FRONT VIEW

The Cuban Rhythm Step

The Cuban Rhythm Step is similar to the Cuban Walk. Whereas the Cuban Walk is merely a slow walking step taken forward, backward or sideward, and the count of the walk is slow, slow, the Cuban Rhythm Step is done to the count of—slow, quick, quick.

In the Cuban Rhythm Step, you dance all steps *forward*. The first step is long and slow. The next two steps are short and quick. Try it with the music and listen carefully to the count. Remember, all steps are taken forward.

Slow, quick, quick; slow, quick, quick.

Dance the Cuban Rhythm Step going in the Line of Direction.

Foreign dances do not come naturally to us. Although the Cuban Rhythm Step is a simple one, it will take several hours of practice before you can do it with ease and confidence.

THE LINE OF DIRECTION

The Line of Direction is the direction dancers should follow in their progress around the room. Practice it this way. The Man begins with the left foot and walks forward around the room. The Girl should practice walking backward, going in the same direction. The Man's right hand and the Girl's left hand should be nearest the wall.

If you do not follow the Line of Direction, you are going "against the grain," and you will run into other couples.

First Half of the Rumba Box Step

THE BOX STEP is the most popular of all the Rumba steps. You'll be amazed to find how easy it is to dance the Rumba after you learn this basic movement.

MAN'S PART
READ UP

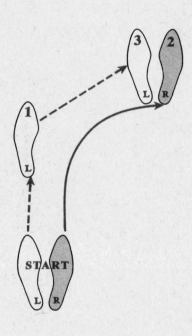

START

1. Begin with left foot and step directly forward.

2. Step diagonally forward to right.

3. Draw left foot up to right foot, heels together.

Second Half of the Rumba Box Step

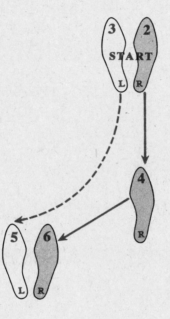

START

4. Step straight back with your right foot.

5. Step to left side with your left foot.

6. Bring your right foot up to your left.

The Girl's part is the same as the Man's.

The Box Step in the Rumba

THIS IS a combination of the two previous pages.

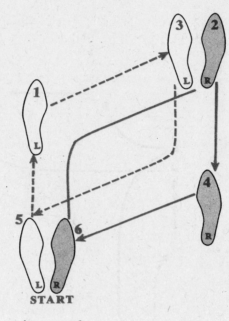

MAN'S PART

START

Start with your feet together

1. Left foot forward (slow).

  2. Right to right side (quick).

    3. Left up to right (quick).

4. Right foot back (slow).

  5. Left to left side (quick).

    6. Right up to left (quick).

    The complete Box Step is the basis for the Left Turn and must be practiced for at least an hour with music.

The Left Box Turn in the Rumba

ONCE YOU are thoroughly familiar with the Box Step . . . learning to turn is easy. All the steps are exactly the same as in the Box Step.

To do the left turn, you simply do the Box Step, but on the *first* count you *turn* slightly to your *left*.

MAN'S PART

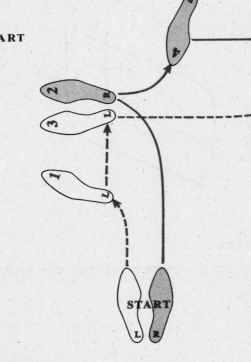

Looking over your left shoulder:

1. Step *forward* on left and turn left.

2. Right to side.

3. Left up to right.

4. Step back on right.

5. Left to side.

6. Right up to left.

NOTE: Be sure you are thoroughly familiar with all these Rumba steps before you attempt the Rumba Breaks on the following page.

The Rumba Breaks

THE MOST interesting variations in the Rumba are the Breaks. The Breaks may be done forward, backward, or to either side.

THE FORWARD BREAK
1. Step forward with left foot (slow).
2. Bring right foot up to left (quick).
3. Step in place with left foot (quick).

Note that the count in the Rumba is slow, quick, quick.
Repeat pattern starting with right foot progressing forward.
4. Forward with right foot (slow).
5. Bring left foot up to right (quick).
6. Step in place with right foot (quick).

THE BACKWARD BREAK
1. Step back with left foot (slow).
2. Bring right foot back to left (quick).
3. Step in place with left foot (quick).

THE SIDE BREAKS

The Side Breaks are done in the same manner and to the same count as the Forward Break.

Break to Left Side:
1. Step to side with left foot (slow).
2. Bring right foot up to left (quick).
3. Step in place with left (quick).

Break to Right Side:
4. Step to side with right foot (slow).
5. Bring left foot up to right (quick).
6. Step in place with right (quick).

Remember that each step is given two beats of music, and each quick step one beat of music. This means a total of four beats to a bar of Rumba music.

COMBINATION OF BOX STEP AND SIDE BREAK

Master the Box Step as shown in the diagram on page 118.

1. Left forward (slow).
2. Right to side (quick).
3. Draw left up to right (quick).
4. Step back on right (slow).
5. Left to side (quick).
6. Draw right up to left (quick).

Practice the above Box Step for fifteen minutes before adding the Side Breaks:

1. Left foot to left side (slow).
2. Place right foot *behind* left (quick).
3. Step in place with left (quick).
4. Right foot to right side (slow).
5. Place left foot behind right (quick).
6. Step in place with right foot (quick).

Note that as you place one foot behind the other on the second count, the dancers separate.

The Arthur Murray Turn

THE ARTHUR MURRAY Turn is styled for both fast and slow Rumba music.

Before attempting the Turn, learn the pattern of the step.

MAN'S PART

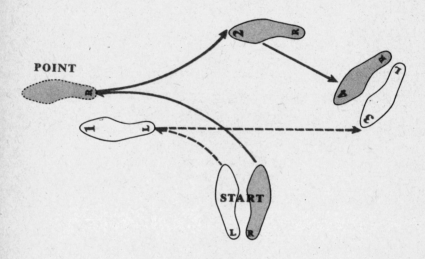

POINT

START

1. Step forward on the left foot and point the right foot in front.

2. Step back on right foot.

3. Place left foot to left side.

4. Bring the right foot up to the left.

Now repeat the step, practicing with music.

To do the Arthur Murray Turn, as described on the preceding page, you merely turn to the left as you step forward on the left foot on the first count.

It will help you in turning, if, as you step forward on the left foot, you look over your left shoulder.

NOTE: Look over your left shoulder as you step forward on your left foot.

The Open Break in the Rumba

THE MOST interesting and intricate-looking steps in the Rumba are very simple when analyzed—for instance, the Open Break, which is a combination of a half Box Step and a Backward Break. The half Box Step is described on page 116. After doing a half Box Step, the Man steps back on his left foot and brings his right foot quickly back to the left.

On the Break, he releases the Girl's hand, so that, as she steps back on her right foot (and brings her left quickly back to her right), she swings away from her partner. Notice the illustration on this page.

You will have no difficulty in mastering this, or any other of the novelty Rumba steps after you become expert in the Box Step and the Breaks as taught in these lessons.

A REVIEW OF THE RUMBA STEPS

Although it is not necessary to dance the Rumba steps in the following sequence, it will be good practice to master them. If you can dance them without missing a step, you may then do the various Rumba steps in any order you please. When each step is called simply follow the instructions. Accept this challenge and you will find that doing the Rumba is exciting.

1. Stand up with heels together and get ready to do the basic Box Step. Start with your left foot. *Forward, side, together . . . back, side, together.*
2. Now the Cuban Rhythm step . . . all steps are taken forward, and the count is Forward, two, three, slow, quick, quick.
3. Now the Forward Break. Step forward with left foot; bring right foot up to left (quick); step in place with left foot (quick).
4. And now the Arthur Murray Turn.

The Tango

FOR MANY years, the Tango has been danced by professionals in a very elaborate manner. They have made it appear to be a difficult and complicated dance. As a result of seeing such exhibitions, many people have felt that the Tango was far beyond their ability, and have therefore been reluctant to try it.

The original Tango, which came from the Argentine, *was* a difficult step, and the French adaptation of it was almost as difficult. The Americanized version, however, is a very simple ballroom dance which you should have no trouble at all in learning.

The steps are somewhat similar to those used in the Waltz and the Fox Trot, and I have arranged the Tango here so that anyone who has mastered these dances will be able to go on easily to the Tango.

The *deliberate* manner in which the Tango is danced will enable you to develop very quickly the necessary co-ordination between mind and feet. And the poise, balance, and sense of rhythm that this beautiful step will give you will enhance all your dancing.

This new Tango is often called the "Waltz Tango" because of the predominance of old-fashioned Waltz steps in it. In order to become an expert Tango dancer, you must first have a thorough grounding in Waltz routines.

Tango Rhythm

As I explained to you, the rhythm of Tango music is similar to that of the Fox Trot, but it is usually played much more slowly.

The steps are divided into *slow* and *quick* movements.

The *slow* step takes about a second and is given *two beats* of the music.

The *quick* step is twice as fast as a slow step, and it is given only *one beat* of the music.

The slow steps are held quite long, but the quick steps are taken exactly on time with the music, in order to make a pronounced contrast between the two. This slow-quick variation is what gives the Tango a great deal of its individuality and charm.

The Tango Promenade

GENERALLY SPEAKING, the Tango walking step is not very different from the one you have already learned in the Fox Trot. Tango steps though, even in a ballroom version, should have something of the long, swinging, graceful strides of the hard-riding Gauchos who originated the dance in the pampas country.

There are two points to remember in the Tango walking step:

1. Place one foot directly in front of the other and turn the toes *out*.
2. As you step forward with one foot, bring the other foot forward after it with a long, easy motion. Swing the shoulder opposite to the forward-moving foot in a forward direction. (Left foot forward—right shoulder forward, etc.)

Now practice the Tango walking step as follows:

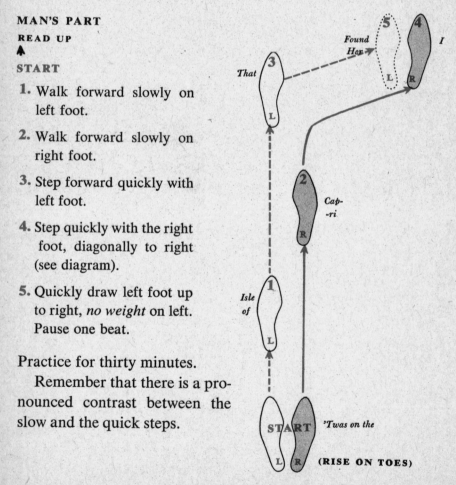

MAN'S PART

READ UP

START

1. Walk forward slowly on left foot.

2. Walk forward slowly on right foot.

3. Step forward quickly with left foot.

4. Step quickly with the right foot, diagonally to right (see diagram).

5. Quickly draw left foot up to right, *no weight* on left. Pause one beat.

Practice for thirty minutes.

Remember that there is a pronounced contrast between the slow and the quick steps.

For the purpose of this lesson, I have chosen the well-known Tango Fox Trot, "Isle of Capri." If you are not familiar with it, you will have no difficulty in finding someone who can sing the first line for you: " 'Twas on the Isle of Capri that I found her."

Sing this line aloud, and make each step correspond to the words printed alongside the footprint.

GIRL'S PART
READ DOWN

'Twas on the

(RISE ON TOES)

START

Isle
of

1. Walk slowly backward on right foot.

2. Take a long, *slow* step backward on left foot.

3. Step directly backward quickly with right foot.

4. Left foot diagonally to left quickly.

5. Draw right foot up to left, quickly, *no weight* on right.

Cap-
-ri

That

I   *Found*
         Her

The El Sharon Promenade

THIS IS the most popular Tango step in the Arthur Murray Studios. It may be done several times without changing to another variation, yet it always looks fresh and sprightly.

MAN'S PART

READ UP

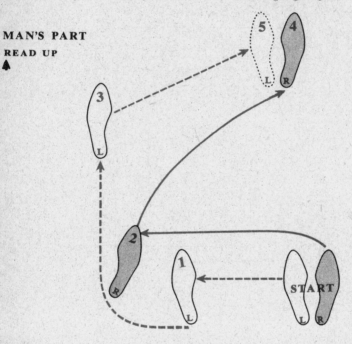

1. Slow step with left foot to left.
2. Cross right foot in front of left (slowly).
3. Quick step forward with left foot.
4. Quick step to right with right foot.
5. Draw left up to right, no weight on it.

NOTE: On the second step the Man crosses his right foot in *front* of his left so that he is *brought to the side of his partner* instead of in front of her.

Also note that the left foot on the fifth step carries no weight.

To obtain a better appreciation of your own part, it is advisable
to learn the Man's part first.

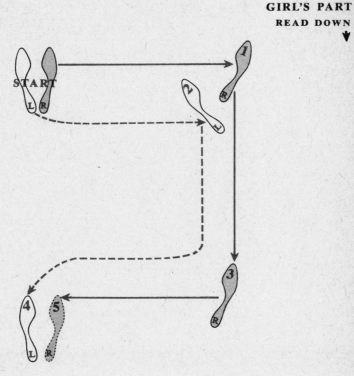

GIRL'S PART
READ DOWN
▼

1. Slow walking step to right on right foot.
2. Slow step back with left, crossing it *behind* right.
3. Quick step back on right foot.
4. Left foot to side.
5. Draw right foot up to left, no weight on it.

131

The Promenade Corté in the Tango

MAN'S PART

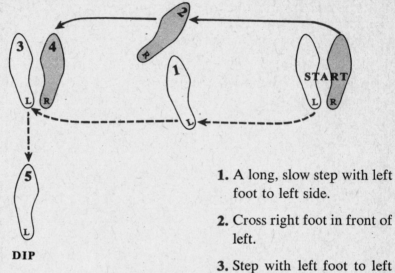

1. A long, slow step with left foot to left side.

2. Cross right foot in front of left.

3. Step with left foot to left side.

4. Draw right foot up to left.

5. Step back on left, dip, bend left knee.

ALL THE STEPS are taken sidewise except the last, on which you corté or dip. The Man has his back to the center of the room as he progresses to his left.

The first two steps are slow; the last three are done quickly, dipping back on the last step.

The Argentine Walk

THIS IS the most typical of all Tango steps. The first three steps are taken quickly. Number four is slow. It requires a great deal of practice to do the third step quickly, in time to the music.

1. Long step forward with left foot.

2. Long step forward with right foot.

3. Step forward with left foot.

4. Step to right with right foot (see diagram).

Repeat step from the beginning.

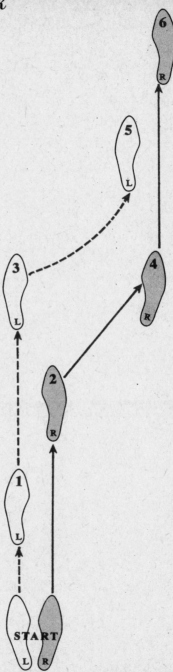

133

The El Sharon Promenade

The Argentine Walk

TANGO ROUTINE NUMBER ONE

Tango Promenade	Once
El Sharon	Twice
Tango Promenade	Once

REPEAT

TANGO ROUTINE NUMBER TWO

Tango Promenade	Once
Argentine Walk	Three Times
El Sharon	Once

REPEAT

Practice Routines Numbers One and Two together.

The Tango Promenade

The Samba

FROM THE throbbing tropics of Brazil come the pulsating rhythms of the Samba—one of South America's most popular dances. Here is how it originated.

The earliest African slaves in Brazil brought with them a primitive native dance, the *Semba*. But Samba dancing or music was not heard of in Brazilian society until the early part of the last century, when the *Lundu,* an early form of Samba melody, was sung in the court of Dom Pedro I, the first Emperor of Brazil. These *Lundus* were chanted by Chalaca, the Emperor's favorite, at the glittering fêtes of his mistress, the famed beauty Domitila, Marchioness of Santos.

Samba dancing did not reach widespread popularity with members of modern Brazilian society until quite recently. Learning the Samba in its more barbaric forms as danced at Carnival time, they refined it to the more suave mood suitable for ballroom dancing. Dancers incorporated in it some of the voluptuous *Maxixe* that enjoyed international fame three decades ago.

The result is the light-hearted, danceable Samba which has swept up from Brazil to become one of the most popular dance rhythms in America.

The Samba Motion

Stand in place, with weight on toes. Keep feet and knees together. Heels should not touch the floor.

1. Rise up on toes.
2. Drop weight, flexing knees forward.
3. (Same as Number 1.)
4. (Same as Number 2.)

Please note that at no time should your heels touch the floor. Knees should be close together at all times.

The Samba motion is actually easier than it sounds. You simply rise on the first count; come down with knees bent on the second count; repeat.

This slight up-and-down motion is carried through every step of the Samba. It is, therefore, necessary to practice it until it becomes second nature to you.

The Pendulum Step

Swing forward

Starting forward with left foot, take long, sweeping step forward, bring right foot up to left quickly, weight on right, then return weight to left . . . count one and two . . .

Swing backward

Step back with right foot, taking long, sweeping step, bring back left foot quickly to right, weight on left, then shift weight from left to right . . . count three and four.

Keep repeating this for an effective pattern. Remember—the feet lead the body. As the feet go forward, the body sways back, as the feet go back, the body sways forward—an easy, rocking step, a graceful, swaying movement.

The Half Turn—Meia Volta

or Rhythm Turn

Weight forward on left foot,
body leaning slightly to left,
using left foot as pivot, give
short pushes with right foot
as you go round . . .

Count one and two and three
and four . . .
Shift weight to right foot and
repeat, for a reverse turn.

The Full Turn—Volta Completa

Step forward with left foot, body weight over left, lead arm down. Give short push with right foot, return weight to left . . .
count one and two
Step back on right foot, shooting lead arm up over head in arc, throwing weight back over right foot. Give short push with left foot, then return weight to right . . .
count three and four

Let the body lead the turns for free, swaying movement. The arms lead the Full Turn in a continuous circular sweep, the body swaying as you shift your weight from left to right, from right to left, with easy abandon and grace.

The Balancetes

To the left

1. Step to side with left foot.

2. Place right foot in back of left, weight on right.

3. Step in place on left.

4. Right foot to right side.

5. Place left foot behind right, weight on left.

6. Step in place on right. Repeat four times!

To the right

Come, dance the Samba! It's easier than the American Two Step, and lots more fun. A gay, lilting dance, joyous as the spirit of Rio at Carnival time. Start a Samba record—catch the simple one-two, one-two rhythm—catch the easy backward, forward movements.

141

The Copacabana

- Step forward with left foot, weight on left, and bending knees so that body is tipped slightly back.
- Take back step on right foot, reaching for the back step so that right knee straightens . . . count one and two . , .
- Step on left foot, and straighten knees, bringing body upright . . . count three and four.

Practice this step until you are sure of it. Then reverse the step, and practice stepping forward on the right foot.

The Reverse Copacabana

- ▶ Three side Balancetes (see page 141) starting to left, releasing partner to open position on the third.
- ▶ Then starting on right foot, take three Copacabana steps forward.
- ▶ Now, forward with left foot turning to left.
- ▶ Right foot to right side. Draw left foot to right.
- ▶ Back with right foot. Left foot to left side.
- ▶ Draw right foot to left . . .
- ▶ Count one and two and three and four.

When you learned the Samba rhythm, you can dance this step any way you want. And now that you know the Samba, invite your partner to dance—in true Brazilian fashion.

The Mambo

A VERY exciting variation of the Rumba is now very popular—the Mambo. The Mambo is to Rumba what Jitterbug or Swing is to Fox Trot.

THE FIRST HALF OF BASIC MAMBO STEP

MAN'S PART
READ UP

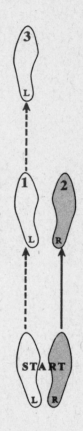

START

1. Step directly forward on left.

2. Draw right foot up to left.

3. Step forward with left, accenting with left foot.

Note that Step 1 is done slowly; 2 and 3 are taken quickly. This is the standard Arthur Murray way of counting the Rumba or Mambo.

THE SECOND HALF OF BASIC MAMBO STEP

4. Step back with right foot.

5. Draw left up to right.

6. Step back with right foot,
accenting with right foot.

After mastering the Mambo steps forward and backward, combine them and practice

THE MAMBO TURN

To turn, simply repeat the above, but as you step forward and backward, turn to left on the first of every three counts. (Keep turning to left only.)

After you have thoroughly mastered the Basic Mambo step, try releasing your partner in the Mambo Break, illustrated above.

PART FIVE

SWING

Swing

AND NOW we come to the dance that spells youth, vitality and the sheer joy of living more than all other dances. It's as bubbling and effervescent as champagne! Whether it's called Swing, Lindy or Jitterbug, it's one of our most exciting dances.

Dancers in different parts of the country adopt their own local variations, but all Swing steps are similar in character and rhythm.

BASIC LINDY STEP

The Basic Lindy Steps can be done in three different rhythms. All these rhythms are equivalent, in count, to a Waltz danced to Fox Trot music. In other words, one slow step, and two quick steps.

Here is easiest Lindy step—the Single Lindy. Don't try to learn the steps on the next few pages until you are thoroughly familiar with this basic step.

1. Step left (slow)

2. Step right (quick)

3. Step left (quick)

4. Step right (slow)

5. Step left (quick)

6. Step right (quick)

NOTE: The quick steps can be taken back-forward, forward-back, or back-together. Any of these ways are correct.

The Double Lindy Hop

First Half to Left

1. Tap in place with left foot (no weight on left).

2. Step to left with left foot.

3. Bring right foot up to left, weight on right.

4. Step in place with left foot, weight on left.

Second Half to Right

1. Tap in place with right foot (no weight on right).

2. Step to right, on right foot.

3. Bring left foot up to right, weight on left.

4. Step in place with right foot, weight on right.

Girl's part: Same as Man's, starting on right foot.

The Triple Lindy Hop

First Half to Left

1. Step to left with left foot, and bring right foot up to left.

2. Step in place with left foot. (These are all quick steps. The three steps require two beats of music and can be counted one-and-two.)

3. Slow step in place with right foot.

4. Slow step in place with left foot.

Second Half to Right

1, 2. Repeat steps 1 and 2, starting to right with right foot.

3. Step back with left foot.

4. Step forward on right foot.

The count for the Girl's part is the same as the Man's; she, naturally, starts on the right foot and steps to the right.

150

The Sugar Foot Walk
in the Lindy Hop

WHENEVER PARTNERS separate, on the two slow steps the Girl does the Sugar Foot Walk as follows:

Begin with left foot.

    1. Step forward on toe, heel turned in.

    2. Quickly turn heel out. This is a quick motion of the foot.

REPEAT with right foot.

The Tuck-In-Turn

1.

2.

USING Double Lindy Rhythm, on counts one and two, Man turns Girl in to face his right side. (See illustration No. 1.)

On counts three and four, the Man makes a complete turn to his left as he spins the Girl to her right. (See illustration No. 2.)

Finish with second half of Double Lindy step. (See instructions on page 149.)

152

PART SIX

DANCE SECRETS

BY

KATHRYN MURRAY

How Many Steps Should a Good Dancer Know?

THERE ARE many answers to this question. The average dancer must consider not only his own point of view, but also his partner's. If a man knows only a few steps and repeats them over and over, his partner naturally tends to lose interest. If a girl is unable to follow skillfully the steps her partner takes, she can hardly expect to be a much-sought-after dancing companion.

The beginner, however, should not concern himself too much with variety, but he must learn all the basic steps given in this book. These are the absolute minimum. Once you have mastered them, all the variations will be easy. But remember that any one of these variations, unless mastered thoroughly, will later cause you to make frequent mistakes, which will lead your partner to question your ability and lose confidence in you.

The good dancer can vary his steps as he pleases. The good dancer, with his perfect knowledge of the basic steps and their combinations—can, with a little ingenuity, improvise many combinations of steps of his own in addition to the ones taught in this book.

But a dancer should never sacrifice perfection for variety.

A dancer has to build up his repertoire slowly, and he should not attempt elaborate steps until he has perfected the simpler ones.

In the final analysis, remember that you dance for pleasure—your own as well as your partner's—and the greater variety of steps you command, the more fun there will be for both members of the team. PROVIDED YOU DANCE THE STEPS WELL!

Helpful Hints for Tall Girls

ONE CHARACTERISTIC that is admired in American girls is their height and fine bearing. Whereas most short girls yearn to be taller—few tall girls would trade places with them. Tall girls should be proud of their size; they should remember that models, who are selected for beauty of appearance, are always well above average height.

However, short men do avoid dancing with girls who tower above them. They are afraid of looking insignificant and comic— even when they secretly admire the girl's appearance.

Tall girls can be smart — they can seem shorter to partners whenever they choose. Here are two pointers that work:

1. KEEP YOUR ELBOWS LOW when you dance. You will appear shorter because your partners will not have to reach upward for dancing position. But, practice this with your girl friends first so you can avoid resting your arms heavily on your partner.
2. Without changing your natural standing posture in any way, LET YOUR KNEES BEND SLIGHTLY. This will reduce your height by several inches. Practice in private!

Perhaps you will feel that these suggestions do not improve your appearance. But, if I were a girl, and had to choose between pleasing my partner or the onlookers, I wouldn't hesitate for a moment. I'd forget my appearance, if need be, and stand so that my partner would feel comfortable and would want to dance with me again.

Bent knees, by the way, will not show with long skirts.

DANGERS FOR TALL GIRLS TO AVOID

Tall girls should never try to appear smaller by leaning forward. This will make you difficult to lead, whether your partner

155

is tall or short. Your hips and feet will be too far apart from your partner's and you will not only look, but feel awkward in all steps. It is an impossible position in which to follow turning steps.

Do not take short steps. No matter how tall you are, you can never take too long a step. Don't worry—your partner's right hand will act as a safety brake.

Be proud of your height—and carry it proudly!

Keep your elbows low.

Let your knees bend slightly.

156

Helpful Hints for Small Girls

LITTLE GIRLS often complain about their lack of height—but they never remember the advantages they have. Just think of it—no partner is ever the wrong size. Men of all sizes are possible partners.

Even the smallest girl, whose vision is bounded by vest buttons, can be a comfortable, adjustable partner to a six-foot-plus. Here are confidential hints to pint-sizers:

1. Train yourself to dance on the tips of your toes instead of balancing your weight on the soles of your feet. Practice this, at home and alone, until you can stretch and reach smoothly.

2. Always imagine that you are trying to touch the ceiling with the top of your head. Stretch high up, from the waist, to gain height.

3. Here is the most valuable tip of all: LEAD WITH YOUR TOES! You can actually see in your mirror that by reaching back, with your big toe leading, that you have lengthened your step from four to six inches. By doing this, your steps will be as long as those taken by a girl five inches taller than you are.

4. Hold your elbows as high as you can. Practice alone, holding your arms bent in partner position—as high up as possible. Exaggerate—and your muscles will be strengthened and ready for the real thing.

5. Always hold firmly with your left hand at the back of your partner's shoulder. No matter how hard you grip—

it will be welcome to him. All men find it easier to lead a girl who holds firmly to their right shoulders.

6. Never take short steps. Practice until you can step forward, backward and to each side with a long, graceful stride (toes leading).

Dance on the tips of your toes and take long steps.

Dancing Don'ts

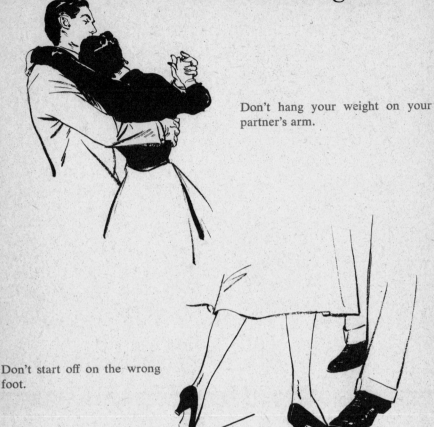

Don't hang your weight on your partner's arm.

Don't start off on the wrong foot.

- DON'T start off on the wrong foot! The man always starts with his left foot—the girl with her right. Easy? Sure, if you know your left from your right.
- DON'T (girls) hang your full weight on your partner's arm; he can't dance for both of you. Balance on your own two feet and support your own weight. If you can't, then stay home and take your vitamins.
- DON'T (men) walk forward all of the time. Your partner will get mighty tired of backing up all evening. Try strolling backward for five minutes straight and you'll get the idea.

159

Don't criticize your partner's dancing.

Don't make your back steps too short.

▶ DON'T criticize your partner's dancing . . . this goes for both sexes. Finding fault with the other fellow is a sure sign of a beginner—or worse, of a sourpuss.

▶ DON'T (girls) always blame your crushed toe on your partner. Maybe your back steps are too short. Test yourself—are the toes of your new slippers soiled already? Then, practice long steps, stretching back with your toes. Get out of his way!

▶ DON'T be a sad-eyed Sammy or a sour-apple Sue. The dance floor is a place for fun; do your worrying on your own time. Smile now, or you're apt to have no one to smile with.

160

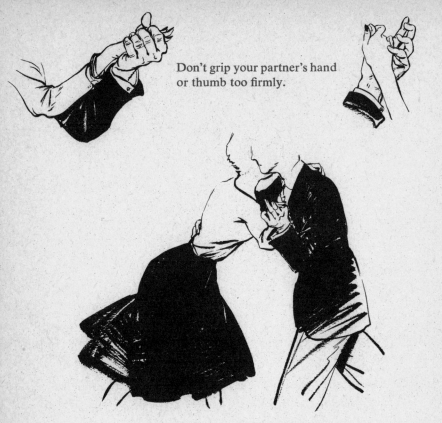

Don't grip your partner's hand
or thumb too firmly.

Don't dance with your hips way back.

▶ DON'T (girls) believe for a minute that all you have to do is relax.
To relax is to collapse. Be alert, full of pep, on your toes—then
you'll be fun to dance with!

▶ DON'T forget that the best position for dancing is the same as for
walking—keep erect. Dancing with hips way back is out of date.
Besides, remember the stag line's view; you owe something to
your public!

▶ DON'T clutch your partner's hand too firmly. You may not know
your own strength. And, girls, don't take a death grip on the poor
man's thumb; you've got him safely hooked for the dance—he
can't get away.

Don't be a butterfly.

▶ DON'T hum or sing loudly. Remember that you're only an inch from your partner's ear. Humming or singing is fine if you're good enough to compete with the orchestra. But if you aren't sure of the tune or the words, do your warbling in the shower.

▶ DON'T (girls) be butterflies. You have arms, not wings. A loose hold will make you miss the lead and stumble. What a comedown that will be! Hold your left hand in a firm grip on the back of your partner's shoulder—you'll keep your balance and your partner's praise.

▶ DON'T hug the floor! LIFT YOUR FEET! Lift your feet a fraction of an inch off the floor and move them through the air. Air offers no resistance—therefore, you can step lightly and effortlessly. Lift your feet slightly for graceful dancing.

▶ DON'T keep apologizing. When you make a mistake say, "I'm sorry"—but just say it once. If you protest: "Gee, I'm clumsy" too often, someone may believe you.

Don't go to extremes.

DON'T go to extremes. A stately tread belongs in marble halls; bouncing high is for the village green. They are both too exaggerated for present-day dancing.

Dancers used to hop high in the days of the Gallop, Polka and Leaping Waltz. Then, fashions changed and swung far the other way. Dancing became overly conservative, dignified. Every step seemed meticulously measured.

With this vogue for dignity, in about 1900, came the theory that good dancers must not lift their feet. Dancing teachers of the day preached: "Do not permit a crack of light to show between your feet and the floor."

This certainly made for dull dancing. How can you dance lightly, with expression and animation, when your feet scrape the floor? The answer is: you can't. So you must lift your feet while you dance, but take it easy.

Exercises to Improve Your Dancing
(For Girls)

AT EVERY newsstand you will find books of instructions for playing tennis, golf, swimming, and so on. This information is easy to read and digest—but do you feel that you could perform these muscular activities just by knowing about them?

Dancing deals with the muscles, too. You can pick up steps just by watching them, or reading their description, but you will have your knowledge in your head only. Your feet and your body cannot respond to your will and desire alone; your muscles must first be trained to obey your command.

Men who want to be good dancers must learn only their own part, and train their muscles to follow the steps they choose to do. But girls are in a different position: they must be able to follow many partners, some tall, some short; some with a great variety of intricate steps, some with a weak lead and faltering steps.

The way to become an alert, agile partner is to train your muscles to obey quickly and to strengthen them to support you in any direction you choose to move.

You cannot dance merely by wanting to—any more than you can be a fine tennis player just because you know the rules and know that the game is fun to play.

To exercise sufficiently takes character and determination. It takes enthusiasm, too. If you really want to be a far better than average dancer, you will study these exercises carefully. They are a sure means of training your dancing muscles quickly and effectively. Remember, no one can do it for you, but once you've achieved your ambition to be an attractive, popular partner, everyone will envy you.

Here are eight exercises for girls. You will find it more entertaining to do them in front of your mirror, in time to music.

EXERCISE 1

Have you ever wondered why some girls look better standing than others do? Or, have you ever wished that you knew how to stand when someone takes your snapshot?

Count One of this exercise will give you the same standing posture that the best photographers' models use. Count Two will give you the backstep technique of an exhibition dancer.

To make your feet look well as you stand, train your heels to always come together—as in the illustration. The toes should be turned out and the knees should touch each other. Look in your mirror!

On the count of one, bring your heels together so that your knees touch and your toes point outward. Now, on the count of two, kick your right foot as far back as possible—toe pointed out and leading. Return to correct position of count one. Repeat this same movement with your left foot and continue in time to slow Fox Trot music.

EXERCISE 2

This is an exercise that will train your feet and ankles to look attractive from any angle. It will teach you automatically to turn your toes outward—a definite "must" for any girl who wants to look well while dancing.

Place your feet together as in Exercise 1. Take a peek in your mirror to see how you're doing. Then, step backward with your left foot, counting one—draw your right foot up to your left, counting two.

Now try the same thing with your right foot back.

Repeat this movement, going backward around the room. Don't forget that your toes must be turned outward.

This back step may seem exaggerated to you, but remember that most of your partners are going to walk you backward very often. You must prepare your muscles to carry you easily.

EXERCISE 3

The illustration shows the finished product of this exercise. If you find it difficult to keep your balance, don't be discouraged—it merely proves that you need the practice. It will come easily after a few tries.

This is glamour training—it will develop supple muscles in your diaphragm and waistline.

Stand with your heels together, and your hands held loosely at your sides.

Step sideways on your right foot to the right, and draw your left foot behind the right, as you see in the correct illustration. At the same time, bring your arms and hands up in the position shown. Sway to the right.

Then step with your left foot to the left and bring your right foot up to and in back of your left. Sway to the left.

It is helpful to practice this to slow Waltz music, using three counts for each swaying movement—one, two, three to right; four, five, six to left.

EXERCISE 4

When you first try this exercise, you may feel insecure. If so, lean on the top of your dresser or on the back of a chair until you can hold your balance.

This movement will train you to hold your head up high and it will gracefully arch your back. A stiff, unyielding back makes a girl feel wooden to her partner.

Begin by standing erect, with your hands at your sides and your heels together. Then swing into the position shown in the correct illustration.

Repeat, swinging back on the other foot.

This can be practiced to slow Waltz music or by counting one, two, three. Don't bring your feet together again until after the third beat.

Note that the toes of the back-swinging foot are leading—and pointing outward.

CAUTION: Do not repeat these exercises too often the first time —or you will regret it the next day!

EXERCISE 5

If you can do this exercise correctly, with your body erect, you will develop a good sense of equilibrium. Practice it until you are well satisfied with your appearance in your mirror.

Simply extend one foot to the side and raise it as high as possible as shown in the illustration. Note that—again—your toes should lead.

Practice this ten times with one foot and then repeat to the other side.

When you have mastered this, with good balance and keeping your body erect, then rise on the toes of the foot carrying the weight.

Count: one, two, three, four. Raise foot, one, two. Lower foot, three, four. Try it to slow Fox Trot music.

This exercise will not only train you in balancing, but it will enable you to follow any quick side step that a partner may take.

EXERCISE 6

Do your knees crra-ack as you bend? You can oil them with this exercise—it's meant to overcome stiff knee joints. It will help you to take smooth dancing steps, rather than the jerky movements of a beginner.

To begin: stand up straight in a natural position.

Take a long forward step with your right foot and place the weight on that foot. Bend the right knee and, keeping your body erect, bend as far down as possible.

Not so easy? The results will be worth it—try again.

After bending, rise and resume your standing position. Now, without moving out of place, step forward with your left foot—weight on that foot—and bend as before.

Do this exercise gradually, a few times a day at first, or you may need rubbing oil for your knees!

If you are practicing to music, allow three beats of a Waltz for the downward bend and three beats to rise to place.

EXERCISE 7

Girls who are not good dancers always dread dancing forward, toward their partners. It makes them feel insecure, clumsy—and they are in fear of stumbling over the man's feet.

Good dancers must be able to glide forward easily. In the Waltz, for instance, almost half the girl's steps will be toward her partner. This exercise will give you the security and confidence that you need; practice it.

Without bending your body forward, raise your right foot until it is parallel with the floor. Stretch your toes out—not up.

To develop dancing poise, hold your foot up for about five seconds, then lower it slowly. Repeat ten times, then try it with the other foot.

EXERCISE 8

It puzzles a man when he finds that some big, stout girls are easy and light to lead—while a slender one-hundred pounder may be as heavy as lead.

If you want to hear a man say to you: "You're wonderful to dance with—you're as light as a feather," then train your arms. This exercise will do it—and furthermore, it will add to your balance and poise.

Rise up on your right toe, raising your left leg backward, as high as you can. Let your toes lead and point outward. At the same time, bring your right arm up in the position shown in the picture. Hold this graceful pose for three beats of a Waltz measure, then slowly lower your hands and feet.

IMPORTANT: Always make your wrists lead when using your arms and hands.

How to Express
Your Personality in Your Dancing

IN A WHOLE roomful of dancers, did you ever spot one person whom you wished could be your partner? You'll notice that it isn't appearance alone that attracts you. There is another quality that draws your attention like a magnet. Call it "charm" or "personality"—however you describe it, it shows in everything you do.

You can develop that extra something that will make your dancing personality colorful, attractive. It's easy, once you know the tricks that will do it.

First of all, accent your dancing! Give it highlights. Accent in dancing is a great deal like accent in speaking. A person who talks in a flat, level, unvarying voice is a bore to listeners. He may know a great deal and have a fine vocabulary at his command but it all goes to waste because of his dreary, droning voice.

A man may know a great variety of steps and yet be a dull dancing partner. He must learn to accent his dancing to give it life and pep. Girls, too, must accent the beat and rhythm of the music before they can dance with expression.

To accent in dancing, merely emphasize the same beat of the music that the orchestra does. You can find this most easily by listening for the bass drum beats. Turn on your radio and listen. Note that in a Waltz, the drummer strikes in measures of three beats but that he strikes hardest on each *first* beat.

Practice the Waltz, accenting or emphasizing the first of every three steps. Because a man always starts dancing with his left foot, his first accented step in the Waltz will be taken with his left. A girl will start accenting with her right foot.

It will take a few hours of practice before you can do this easily and automatically. But, it's worth the time—it will make dancing more fun for you, more exciting to your partners and more attractive to onlookers.

THE LAW OF OPPOSITES

Here is a secret of showmanship that will help you to express a sophisticated, smooth dancing personality. I call it the "Law of Opposites," and it is a rule that is used by every good dancer.

When you step forward with either foot, bring your opposite shoulder slightly forward. Look at the picture—note that the girl is stepping forward on her left foot and is turning her right shoulder slightly forward.

Try this movement of the body, while walking toward your mirror. It will remind you of the graceful, controlled steps that a high-diver takes on a springboard. Follow the rule of opposites in your dancing—it gives strength and assurance to the personality that you show.

No dancer can attract partners by body and foot motion alone. The face must dance, too. Remember this—you are not dressed for dancing until you put on a smile! Show the cheerful side of your character when you dance—it will be contagious to your partner and to everyone who watches.

How to Judge
Character by Dancing

As WE watch various couples walk out on the dance floor, we often think to ourselves: "I wonder what sort of people they are." Within a very few minutes we have our answer. For very quickly such traits as timidity, aggressiveness, consideration of others, arrogance, and such characteristics reveal themselves when people dance.

There are those who love themselves—can you spot them? They point their toes too gracefully and meticulously, stepping very carefully indeed. And why shouldn't they take good care of the ten little tootsies that are THEIRS!

The "cuddly couples" are fun to watch—unless you're related to them! Dance floor petters never outgrow the urge. You can put bells on their toes and wedding rings on their fingers—they'll still cuddle!

Here's one of masculine gender only. He meanders around the floor, pushing his partner into everything that comes his way. He's inconsiderate and thoughtless. Marry his type and life will be one traffic jam after another—with you as the bumper!

Then there are the "casual" ones. The girl, with sloppy "I-don't-care" posture and the man, jes' shufflin' along. She's probably a job-drifter hoping for the divine job with hours from twelve to one—and with an hour off for lunch. When she marries, she'll be a handy gal with a can opener. And her limping hazard? The world owes him a living—you might as well deliver it right to his door.

Know the brand marks of jealousy? The possessive man cups his hand tightly on his partner's back. His posture is crouching, as though ready for a springing pounce. Now the trouble with a jealous gal is that her little ways are so fetching—at first. She clings to her partner's arm like glue, looks up in his eyes with an "aren't-you-wonderful" effect and is so attentive that she goes to his head. But, her husband will have a male secretary if she has anything to say!

Don't look too hard for the timid souls—they'll sink to the floor if you stare at them. The masculine variety has low-slung elbows, an apologetic manner, and a hang-dog expression. He takes faltering steps and barely touches his partner. He's hard to follow

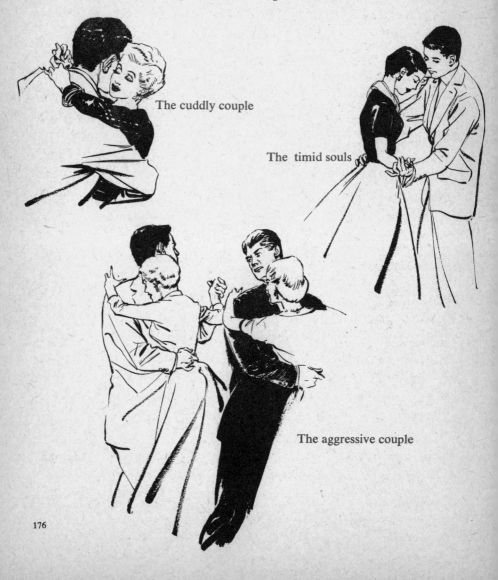

The cuddly couple

The timid souls

The aggressive couple

because he's too shy to lead. The girls of this type take uncertain steps, droop their arms and get an until-death-do-us-part grip on their partner's left thumb.

Beware of the bully—you can spot him on sight. He swings his partner around fast and furiously, with complete disregard for her clothes, hair and general well-being. He turns his toes outward, showing that he is vain as well as self-indulgent.

It takes all kinds to make a world—and you'll find one of each on every dance floor. Watch their steps!

The arrogant couple

The bully

The casual couple

Dance Etiquette

MANY PEOPLE seem to shy away from the word "etiquette." It has an old-fashioned sound. But etiquette, after all, is merely the practical application of good common sense and attractive manners.

Dancing is a partnership and group activity, and so it concerns other people besides yourself. There is never any excuse for faulty manners that might affect or react on others. A popular member of a dancing group is considerate—and shows regard for the comfort and pleasure of partners, a hostess and the other guests.

Once you have accepted an invitation to a dance, you have automatically agreed to live up to the obligations it implies. You are expected to be suitably dressed, to be pleasant company and, above all, to be able to dance.

No one would dream of accepting an invitation for tennis or bridge unless he could play. But many will accept dancing dates when they know quite well that their dancing is not good enough for a partner to enjoy. It's odd, isn't it?

If you can't dance with confidence, have the courage to refuse dancing invitations. Wait until you have the ability and can appear in the best light possible. By starting to practice immediately, you'll be ready and in demand the next time!

A man who accepts an invitation to a dance cannot spend the entire evening with the one partner of his choice. By accepting, he has agreed to add to the festivity of the evening by mingling with the group, by asking several partners to dance, or by changing partners with other couples. Natural courtesy dictates the rule that he must seek out and invite his hostess to dance. If she has daughters or sisters present, they must not be overlooked.

A girl must wait to be asked to dance, but she has her obligations to the party. She cannot, for instance, refuse one partner and then turn around and accept another. Neither should a girl attempt to tie strings to a partner—to hold on to him. She must release him gracefully so that he can get about and dance with others.

When entering or leaving the dance room, the girl always precedes. Men never go first unless they need to do so to give assistance, such as in helping a girl out of a car, bus or so on.

It is no longer considered good taste for a man to take the girl's arm when they are walking to or from the dance floor. This has been out of date for years.

There is a right and wrong way to ask a girl to dance. It puts her in an awkward spot if you say: "Have you the next dance taken?" What girl wants to admit that her dances are not taken! Instead, say: "May I have the next dance?" Don't forget this, it holds true for all invitations. It is more polite to say: "Will you

Don't take the Girl's arm
when walking to or from
the dance floor

go dancing with me on Friday night?" than tactlessly to say: "What are you doing on Friday night?" See the difference?

At the end of each dance, a man must always escort his partner back to where she was sitting. He must never leave her in the middle of the floor. (But, don't forget, he doesn't have to take her by the arm to lead her off!)

When leaving a girl after dancing with her, a man should make some pleasant remark like: "Thank you so much—I enjoyed dancing with you." He should be careful not to say: "I'll be back later," unless he plans to return. A man is well protected by the rules of etiquette. If he has had an uncongenial or dull partner, he can make his exit very smoothly by saying that he must find the girl with whom he has the next dance. Or that he has not yet danced with the hostess.

CUTTING-IN

Cutting-in is an acceptable custom at almost all dances that are held in America. If a man wants to cut-in on the girl of his choice, he should wait until she is dancing fairly near him, at the

Cutting-in is an acceptable custom

Don't refuse to break—
it's bad form

Don't pounce on a new partner with obvious delight

outer edge of the floor. Then he can easily step to her side and nod pleasantly, saying "May I?" to her partner.

It is considered childishly bad form to refuse to "break." Instead, the man who has been cut-in on, should step aside good

181

naturedly, with a slight bow and a smile, and join the stag line. From there, he can do a little cutting-in himself.

There is a generally accepted rule that there must be an intervening cut-in before a man can return to claim his original partner. For instance, if Bill cuts-in on John, John should not cut back on Bill. He should wait until another man is dancing with the girl.

The cut-in system is very cruel to a girl. Even when she likes the partner she has, she yearns for cut-ins, to prove her popularity. But, no matter how welcome the cut is, a girl should not show undue glee. She should smile equally at her original partner and at her new one.

A girl who pounces on a new cut-in with obvious delight makes him wary and suspicious. Further, her stock goes down with a bang because she has been noticeably insulting to her original partner. Neither can she show reluctance to break, even when her original partner is her dream man. Girls must chart their course very carefully for smooth sailing.

CONVERSATION

This is a matter of personality, but there are general rules of good manners to consider. The first taboo is: don't argue! Dancing is a partnership that depends on accord. Two people cannot move as one and enjoy the rhythm of the music together unless they feel harmonious toward each other. So, avoid subjects that might breed discord, such as politics, religion, school elections, and so on. Even when you discuss songs or bands, remember that the sweetest words ever spoken are: "I think you're right!"

There are some people who cannot talk as they dance. Theirs is a companionable silence because it is obvious that their minds are occupied with the rhythm of the music and the pleasure of the dance.

The strong, stern, silent man and the frosty-faced, forbidding female don't belong at a dance. Their partners find them un-

Don't look too stern

Don't spend your dance arguing

Don't talk incessantly

pleasant and the onlookers will avoid them. There may be some reason not to talk as you dance, but always keep your smile on!

The walkie-talkie chatterbox is a conversational hazard, too. There are always a few at every dance; they are so keyed up or so shy that they have forgotten that Silence Is Golden. Their chatter is so steady that it drowns out the loudest band. Like the brook, they ripple on and on. Nothing can be done about it, but you can profit by their example!

INTRODUCTIONS

Introducing people is a bugbear to those who are shy and to those who are young and unpracticed. Actually, the only difficult part is to remember names—and to have them at the tip of your tongue. Otherwise, your cues are easy: you always present the man to the girl, mentioning her name first: "Lillian, this is Mr. Brown—Miss Smith." Or, if you are not on first-name terms with her, you can say: "Miss Smith, may I present Mr. Brown."

When introducing two women, you present the younger one to the older: "Mrs. Jones, this is Miss Smith." If they are of equal age, it doesn't matter which name is mentioned first. "Mrs. Jones—Mrs. Brown."

ACKNOWLEDGING INTRODUCTIONS

It is good training to make a point of remembering names; therefore many people form the habit of acknowledging introductions by repeating the name: "How do you do, Mrs. Brown." If you have not really heard the other person's name, it will flatter them to have you say: "Did you say Mrs. Brown? How do you do."

Don't make the famous mistake that was made by a young girl, who was too shy to ask to have the name repeated—and who, later in the evening, asked: "I'm not quite sure—how do you spell your name?" "S-M-I-T-H, plain Smith," he replied.

Certain replies to introductions have fallen into too common usage and are not considered good taste. As an example: "Pleased to meet you" is no longer used. Yet "I'm so glad to know you" is quite acceptable.

A woman does not rise to acknowledge introductions, unless she is the hostess, or is being introduced to an older person. A hostess rises to greet all of her guests, men or women.

NIGHT CLUB DANCING

So far, we have discussed private dancing parties.

A restaurant, featuring dancing, is quite different. Here your

Avoid complicated steps on a small dance floor

only obligation is to the people of your own party. A cut-in from a stranger should never be accepted, nor should it be offered. A man should avoid leaving his date alone at the table unless it is really necessary. Otherwise, she may be subjected to unwelcome attention.

Most restaurant and night club dance floors are tiny in size, so, in consideration of your partner and your neighbors, you should avoid complicated steps. Dance simply and follow the Line of Direction. This means to progress around the room, clockwise. Shorten your steps to fit the limitation of space.

ONE LAST WORD

It is not bad manners to suggest sitting down before the dance is over: That is, if you suggest the idea tactfully. Either partner can say: "It's warm in here, don't you think so? Shall we sit out and cool off for a few moments?" Or, "It's crowded, isn't it? I'm anxious to talk to you anyway—shall we sit down?"

From now on, try to think more kindly of the word "etiquette" —it protects you, too; don't you think so?

PART SEVEN

DANCING FOR CHILDREN

Why Children Should
Learn How to Dance

WHEN I first began to teach ballroom dancing, I had a class of twenty children in Atlanta, Georgia. How that class grew to a thousand—the largest in the world—is another story; but the fact that of the original twenty many became nationally known leaders proves a very important point.

Mothers and fathers who know their children at home have only a partial picture of their lives. Really to know their children, they must follow them into the classroom and out on the playground. There alone can they tell whether their children are confident young personalities, or stumble over their lessons and edge away from games.

There is nothing more pathetic than the child who stands wistfully looking on while other boys and girls are playing, devoured with eagerness and envy and yet afraid to join in when asked.

Such a child longs for the bell calling him back to class. But in the schoolroom the situation is just as bad. His confusion is so pitiful that he is apt to make Paris the capital of Denmark or the Thames a river in China.

Such a child is not stupid: he is shy. Parents who see only the report card get only the unimportant side of the story.

The child who doesn't mix, and who seems like a dunce in the classroom, needs above all else a good dose of self-confidence and self-assertiveness. Any psychologist will tell you that. But how to administer that dose is another matter. Self-confidence cannot be forced on a child—it has to be administered with a sugar coating.

Years ago, when I worked a great deal with children, I used to have mothers come to me for this sugar coating. "Jane is so shy that she has no little friends," one mother would complain. Another one would tell me about her son, Jack. "I don't understand it, Mr. Murray," she would say. "He's a bright child at home, but I'm actually afraid to let his father see the marks he brings home from school. What shall I do?"

Well, I have had to inject self-confidence into so many youngsters that I feel like an expert. Of course, my sugar coating to the pill is dancing—and it works miracles!

I have seen bashful children cured almost overnight, and the cure was not limited to the dancing class. Just as among adults, being able to dance well gives children a sureness about themselves that carries over automatically into everything else they do.

Children who learn ballroom dancing are taught normal social intercourse at the time when they are the most impressionable pupils. The contacts and courtesies of the dance floor are all to the good, and I have noted that people who learned to dance when they were children have ingrained good manners when they grow up. When people's manners are worn so easily that they seem second nature to them, more likely than not they date from dancing-class days.

I prefer ballroom dancing for children rather than tap, toe, or folk dancing, because it *must* be done with a partner—a fact that attacks shyness at its very roots. A girl who has learned to dance as a child never fades into a wallflower. A boy who learns to dance early in life has "girl-fright" nipped in the bud for him; he is spared from many of the agonies of teen-age self-consciousness. Dancing children, boys and girls, are leaders in the schoolroom and on the playground—and they remain leaders.

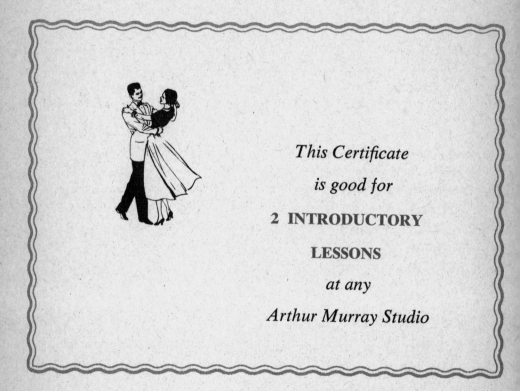

This Certificate

is good for

2 INTRODUCTORY

LESSONS

at any

Arthur Murray Studio